The ER

What Peo₁

"This illuminating book is filled with uncommon sense. Eve Hogan offers a penetrating understanding of what makes relationships great. Anyone who absorbs these rich principles and puts them into action will grow and advance immeasurably in their most important relationships."

— Alan Cohen, author of *Don't Get Lucky, Get Smart*

"*The EROS Equation* puts love back where it belongs; on the top of everyone's priority list! It is the perfect combination of head and heart that adds up to accessing your own genius at love. Hogan's a bonafide relationship connoisseur bent on helping every last one of us find and enjoy true love!"

— Maryanne Comaroto, talk show host of *MaryanneLive!*

"WOW! Seldom do you actually get to read powerful words from someone who actually lives them. Here Eve takes you from where you are to where you must be to actualize life's greatest present— LOVE!"

— Dr. Jeffrey Magee, PDM, CSP, CMC, Publisher
Professional Performance 360 Magazine

"*The EROS Equation* is the ultimate book on relationships and personal growth. This book is a game changer for all of us."

> — Berny Dohrmann, Chairman CEO SPACE
> author of *Redemption: The Cooperation Revolution*

"*The EROS Equation,* Eve Hogan's best work to date, holds the secret for transforming relationships and lives from drama-driven to Spirit-driven, from ego-based to wisdom-based. All this happens in one simple choice to honor our authentic selves—no matter what. Eve is a master at showing us how and has wowed me for years."

> — Lisa Nichols, Author of *No Matter What*

"Creativity is seldom recognized as a critical ingredient for healthy relationships. In *The EROS Equation,* Eve Hogan shares how to tap into our creative spirit to solve problems from higher levels of creative consciousness. A powerful perspective."

> — Barnet Bain, Producer of *What Dreams May Come*
> and *The Celestine Prophecy*, Co-host of *Cutting Edge Consciousness Radio*

"Simple, eloquent, and captivating. I recommend this book highly."

> — Greg S. Reid, Bestselling author/filmmaker

"Eve is truly are an artist of being fully alive and shows us how to make our relationships our masterpieces."

> — Dan Clark, CSP, CPAE Hall of Fame Speaker
> *New York Times* bestselling author

"*The EROS Equation* is amazing! Serious seekers of a passionate, purposeful life must read Eve Hogan's masterful collection of REAL wisdom. This book connects the dots. I'm blown away...and you will be too."

— David M. Corbin, author of *Illluminate: Harnessing the Positive Power of Negative Thinking*

"If you read, listen, and act on the wisdom of this remarkable, well-written, funny, engaging book, you will have transformation. You will have happier relationships, and you will smile more. I sincerely believe that if this book was required reading the world and even the readers of *Spirituality and Health Magazine* would get the transformation that they are asking for."

— Paul Sutherland, Publisher of *Spirituality and Health Magazine*

"Eve's clear and concise way to help you understand the power of Eros, the toxicity of blame and the value of self-responsibility guides the reader to have their best relationship yet."

— Dr. Kevin Ross Emery

DEDICATION

This book is dedicated
to all my teachers, and their teachers
in the many, many forms
they have taken.

Ordering
Trade bookstores in the U.S. and Canada please contact
Publishers Group West
1700 Fourth Street, Berkeley CA 94710
Phone: (800) 788-3123   Fax: (800) 351-5073

For bulk orders please contact
Special Sales
Hunter House Inc., PO Box 2914, Alameda CA 94501-0914
Phone: (510) 899-5041   Fax: (510) 865-4295
E-mail: sales@hunterhouse.com

Individuals can order our books by calling **(800) 266-5592**
or from our website at **www.hunterhouse.com**

THE ER⊕S EQUATION

A "Soul-ution" for Relationships

EVE ESCHNER HOGAN, MA

For further information please contact:
Hunter House Inc., Publishers
PO Box 2914
Alameda CA 94501-0914

Library of Congress Cataloging-in-Publication Data
Hogan, Eve Eschner, 1961-
The EROS equation : a "soul-ution" for relationships /
Eve Eschner Hogan, MA.
pages cm
ISBN 978-0-89793-673-6 (pbk.) — ISBN 978-0-89793-674-3 (ebook)
1. Couples—Psychology. 2. Man-woman relationships. 3. Interpersonal
relations. 4. Love. I. Title.
HQ801.H657 2013
306.7—dc23   2013034073

Project Credits

Cover Design: Brian Dittmar Design, Inc.	Rights Coordinator: Candace Groskreutz
Book Production: John McKercher	Publisher's Assistant: Bronwyn Emery
Developmental Editor: Jude Berman	Customer Service Manager:
Copy Editor: Kelley Blewster	Christina Sverdrup
Managing Editor: Alexandra Mummery	Order Fulfillment: Washul Lakdhon
Publicity Assistant: Martha Scarpati	Administrator: Theresa Nelson
Special Sales Manager: Judy Hardin	IT Support: Peter Eichelberger
Publisher: Kiran S. Rana	

Printed and bound by Sheridan Books, Ann Arbor, Michigan
Manufactured in the United States of America

9 8 7 6 5 4 3 2 1   First Edition   14 15 16 17 18

Contents

Foreword

by JACK CANFIELD

I have known Eve Hogan for over a quarter of a century. I have watched her move from a schoolteacher passionate about helping her students, to a presenter passionate about helping parents and teachers, to a master teacher for the masses. It is impressive to witness someone so dedicated to personal and spiritual growth and to the application of success principles in the realm of relationships.

The EROS Equation is a powerful synthesis of leading-edge concepts compressed into a simple, usable, and immediately applicable form. Eve is able to integrate teachings from a variety of sources with her own experience and wisdom, and present them in a user-friendly manner that simply makes sense.

The EROS Equation is a simple formula that will transform your life. While Eve's emphasis in this book is on relationships, the equation is one of the primary success principles that is key to creating more happiness, success, health, and wealth. This book drives home the simple truth that everything in your life is a result of your choices—choices about what you think, what you read, watch, listen to, what you say, and how you act. Most of us have been conditioned to blame something outside of ourselves for the parts of our lives we don't like. We typically think others *make* us feel bad, or that the things that happen to us are the reason we feel the way we do. We say things like "He made me angry." "She ruined my day." "The kids are driving me crazy." In reality the events in our lives do not cause our feelings or our outcomes. Our responses to those events are what create our results, our experiences, and our solutions.

This book serves as a confrontation with reality. The reality is this: If you keep doing what you have always done, you'll keep on getting what you've always gotten. If you want something different from what you are currently getting, you are going to have to do something different to get it. You need to stop messing around—stop blaming, complaining, and suffering—and start taking responsibility for what you are creating and what you want to create. If you want something different, you have to *do* something different. In order to do something different, you need new information, new methodologies, and new techniques, all of which this book provides. This book offers readers the "something different" to do, in order to shift into high gear and make their lives work better.

When we recognize our responsibility for the current state of our life, we stop playing the blame-and-complain game. We realize that the quality of our lives is up to us. That is the good news, and that is also the bad news.

A few years back, a sixty-five-year-old woman was babysitting her grandson as he was playing in her driveway. She watched in horror as her car, which she thought was securely parked, suddenly rolled backward, pinning him under a back wheel. Without even stopping to think about it, she simply did what needed to be done; she ran over, picked up the back of the car with her bare hands, and freed him. After this heroic event became public, she refused to be interviewed by the media—she stated that she simply didn't want to talk about it. Eventually, a persistent writer managed to get some time with her, but she still didn't want to talk about what she referred to as "the event."

"Why don't you want to talk about the amazing feat you performed to save your grandson?" he asked.

Her reply was thought provoking. "It is very painful for me. When I realized that I was able to pick up that car, which was something I did not believe I could do, I began to wonder what else in my life I might have been able to accomplish if I hadn't thought it was impossible. Being in my sixties I had to ask myself, 'Have I wasted my whole life?'"

After spending a lifetime blaming others or circumstances, it can be a painful experience when we first acknowledge the fact that we are capable, powerful human beings and that the only thing that has ever stood in our way is our belief that we are not. The moment we decide to take responsibility for *everything* in our lives, we are no longer victims. The exhilaration comes as we practice applying our responsibility and we see the new results. We become contagiously happy. Life becomes fun, a game to played, a joy to experience, an adventure to be tackled, a blessing for which to be thankful, rather than a dreary existence to be survived or endured until it is over. The EROS Equation is the method for doing so.

—Jack Canfield

Co-creator of *Chicken Soup for the Soul* series

and coauthor of *The Success Principles*™

 # Acknowledgments

Jack Canfield, thank you for shaking my soul awake to my life's purpose and giving me tools for changing my life and for helping others change theirs.

Berny and September Dohrmann, thank you for giving me such a beautiful place to grow, to learn, and to teach, with so much loving support. CEO Space is the birthplace of nearly all I do and a "home" for which I am so grateful.

To the teens at CEO Space, thanks for being such great teachers.

Lauralyn Eschner, thank you for being not only my sister but also my friend, my editor, and my creative word-crafting consultant! Thank you for adding the "S" to the end of E + R = O. You are a genius!

Al and Meg Eschner, thank you for exposing me to a bigger world of thought and the inner world of divinity—in this life and beyond. You are the role models I would wish for everyone.

Wendy, Amy, and Emily Eschner, thank you for the constant flow of love to and from even in the silent moments in between visits!

Maryanne Comaroto-Raynal, I am eternally grateful for the interchange of ideas, information, self-exploration, and undying love. *You* are my "proof."

Jane Foley, thank you for the thousands of hours spent walking the floors at BEA, brainstorming, learning, encouraging, and supporting.

Tanda and Nahimana Wilson, Kathy Vaughn, Nancy Blackwelder, Suzie Grubler, Marji and Michael Tibbott, Rena and Jon Biel, Janet Baldwin, Sydney Smith, Gail Swanson, Jason Munson, Yinon Scheuer, and all the other amazing people who have assisted and supported me, created beauty, and brought about structure so that I am better able to do this work.

Paul Sutherland and *Spirituality and Health Magazine,* thank you for giving me such a perfectly aligned platform from which to share these principles.

Kiran and Jeanne Rana and Hunter House, you are not just great publishers with a great team; you are great and everlasting friends—my soul family.

Steve Hogan, thank you for all you do, for who you are, for how you are, and for being my life's partner. I love you with all my heart.

Introduction

*Grant me the serenity to accept the things
I cannot change, the courage to change the things I can,
and the wisdom to know the difference.*

— THE SERENITY PRAYER

I originally learned the equation E + R = O from Jack
Canfield, creator of the Chicken Soup for the Soul series, author
of *Success Principles,* and an early mentor in my own personal and
professional growth. Jack learned it from Bob Resnick, one of
his early mentors. E + R = O is one of those timeless concepts that
gets shared like whispered truth among the people lucky enough
to hear it. It is such a powerful idea that it should be shouted from
the rooftops and taught in every school, church, and home. E +
R = O stands for Event + Response = Outcome, which I will fully
explain in the upcoming chapters. In essence, it is a formula for
recognizing that it isn't life's events that cause us pain, suffering,
or joy. Rather, it is our responses to those events that dictate our
experience. Understanding this truth empowers us by helping
us determine what we can change and what we cannot.

Prior to understanding the E + R = O equation, like so many others I looked outside myself for love and validation and for the solutions to my problems. When things went astray in my love life, I blamed "him," whoever "he" was at the time. I just could not figure out how to make relationships work.

When I heard the E + R = O equation, it was as if a part of me clicked into place, like a previously missing puzzle piece. In all of its simplicity and wisdom, the formula offered a structure for me to transform my life. It pushed me to take 100 percent responsibility for my experience (which, admittedly, caused some discomfort at first) and to stop the insanity of blame. As I worked with it, practiced it, experimented with it, I also added to it and built on it. In applying the formula specifically to love relationships, I added the concept of "Solution," thus birthing the EROS Equation:

Event + Response = Outcome & Solution

This is a formula for accessing the power within oneself to resolve problems and create healthy, harmonious, and loving relationships. It also seemed fitting that the Greek word *eros* means "love." In Part Four of the book, I will share with you my personal experience of applying the EROS Equation, and how I know it works.

BLAME LOCKS THE DOOR TO OUR HEARTS

We humans clearly value relationships greatly. We devote huge amounts of time, energy, and money to them. We are all either trying to find one, trying to make one work, trying to get out of one, or trying to recover from one. Our relationships impact how we feel about ourselves, how we succeed in other areas of our lives, how we treat others, and whether or not we are happy. Although love and relationships are among the most important things to nearly everyone, almost no one has been trained in how to make them work.

Humanity suffers from an epidemic of blame. In fact, I have decided that the "original relationship sin" *is* blame. Adam blamed Eve, Eve blamed the snake. When we look outside of ourselves for the source of our problems, we look outside of ourselves for the solutions to our problems. When things go wrong, we typically want the people we are in relationships with to change, certain that if they only behaved differently, we could be happy. When we believe that someone or something else has to change in order for us to be content, we render ourselves victims. This approach simply doesn't work—yet almost everyone does it.

Blame results in anger, hurt, fear, depression, and manipulation. It creates an entire planet of people who feel victimized. People who feel victimized either withdraw, give up, and wither away, or they get angry and seek revenge and retaliation. This painful state of affairs wreaks havoc. Marriages are falling apart at an enormous rate. People are hurting themselves and each other because they can't figure out another way to solve their problems. Blame locks the door to people's hearts.

This way of behaving doesn't make sense. The choices we're making lead us in the wrong direction, as if we were walking due south in the hopes of reaching a destination that lies due north. We have turned the most beautiful experience in the world, that of loving and being loved, into a state of suffering. The suffering has to end. It is time to turn this "relation-ship" around.

CREATING REAL-ATIONSHIPS

In *The EROS Equation,* it is my goal to show you a new perspective on love—one that enables you to create "real-ationships" instead of manning ego battleships.

Real-ationships are not ego driven, but spirit driven. Real-ationships require that we each take 100 percent responsibility for how we show up, how we respond, and the energy we magnetize or attract. Responsibility is the antidote to blame. When we take responsibility for our reactions to events and others, we gain power over our happiness, our relationships, our success—every aspect of our lives.

A lot of confusion exists between the concepts of responsibility and fault. "Fault finding" seeks someone to blame for something that happened in the past. Responsibility is about transcending the ego, recognizing you are not a victim, and taking ownership of your competence. When you do this, you realize your immense capability to experience peace, love, and joy, and to resolve problems in the present, change the course of future events, and heal from the past.

Rather than seeking outside of yourself for love and blaming something outside of yourself for its lack, you can unlock the ability within you to create lasting, loving, joyful relationships—or to get out of one that isn't healthy without carrying its baggage forward.

Although I would love to make everyone feel that what ails them is unique, the reality is that every single person or couple who comes to me for relationship coaching shares a variation on the same problem. I find myself teaching the same skills and tools to everyone, regardless of their individual story. The EROS Equation is the soul-ution to the age-old relationship problem.

The good news is that *only one person in a relationship needs to know how to initiate change.* So don't worry if your partner isn't taking the journey through this book with you. One person shifting can shift the whole relationship.

Consider this: All the elements within a kaleidoscope are always there, a constant. But every time you turn the kaleidoscope you get a different picture. Likewise, all the elements of your relationship may remain unchanged, but when you change the way you look at things and how you interact with your partner, the picture can change dramatically. With every turn, it can become more beautiful.

It may take a week or two to digest the contents of this book, but it takes only one moment—a single turn of the kaleidoscope—to apply its concepts to your love life. One of the best parts of *The EROS Equation* is that the material is immediately applicable to all of your relationships—whether in the home, the workplace, or the larger community. You don't have to wait until you've finished the book to start experiencing results. Each piece of information affords you the opportunity to instantly enhance the joy in your relationships.

HOW THIS BOOK IS STRUCTURED

The book is presented in nine parts:

Part One: The Mythology of Love offers a conceptual framework that will enable you to fully utilize the skills described later in the book. It will also raise your awareness about the impact of your thoughts and beliefs on your relationships.

Part Two: The Common Denominator: You will guide you to strengthening your relationship with yourself. You are the common ingredient in all of your relationships. Love, peace, and happiness all start with you.

Part Three: Ego Battleships vs. Real-ationships will provide you with a deep understanding of what most of us have been doing in relationships, why it doesn't work, and how to begin doing things differently. When you gain an understanding of the ego, its role in relationships, and how to enroll the ego in your soul's agenda instead of the other way around, you become powerful.

Part Four: The EROS Equation fully explains the formula Event + Response = Outcome & Solution and shows you how to use it to transform your relationships. The ability to apply the EROS Equation allows you to become your own best relationship advisor.

Part Five: The Response Options guides you to stop the insanity of "relationships gone bad" by defining effective options for responding to relationship problems.

Part Six: Essential Life and Love Skills outlines six steps that encompass a personal practice for realigning with your authentic self so that your words, thoughts, and actions are pointed toward your goals.

Part Seven: The Guideposts of Integrity helps you to identify your values and your personal code of ethics to guide you on the path of self-mastery.

Part Eight: Managing Emotions and Change reveals the beauty of fear, anger, and hurt as messengers and shows you how to look for their deeper messages, which lead to love. As mentioned, change can happen in an instant, and so can reversion to old habits. Having an understanding of these dynamics will allow you to fully embrace—and master—the process of transformation.

Part Nine: The Soul-ution reminds you to train your brain to start with heart. Within you lies an immense source of wisdom, creativity, discernment, and strength. With every choice you make to access these resources, your life and relationships will be more joyful and harmonious.

You'll note that the term "partner" is used generically throughout *The EROS Equation.* It refers to your significant other or spouse, of course, but also to any relative, friend, coworker, roommate, neighbor, or acquaintance. The tools in this book are applicable to all human relationships, even casual interactions. Two individuals in a relationship, whatever its nature, are "partners" in creating that relationship. They are on the same side, the same team. Ideally, they support each other in the journey of life. Remembering that you are partners or teammates can shift your attitude toward the other person and the relationship, helping you to realize that people generally don't choose to be in partnerships unless they feel that their lives will be enhanced in some way.

You are invited to read the book in sequence the first time. Each chapter builds on the previous one. But please don't feel like you need to wait until you are finished reading to start practicing. Every concept is immediately applicable. Then, keep the book around—in your "reading room" or on the coffee table—as a reminder to implement the tools it offers. Pick a page, any page, and allow yourself to be reminded.

THE INVITATION:
PUT THE EROS EQUATION TO THE TEST

Each chapter concludes with an "Invitation" to apply the chapter's concepts to your life through either journaling or contemplation. The Invitations are simple; they are not lengthy, time-consuming exercises. They are self-directed and revolve around self-inquiry. Should you decide to accept the Invitations, you will improve your ability to generate change, even if all you do is begin to notice *what* you do and *how* you do it.

Self-awareness is the key to change. When we are self-aware, we can see what we are doing rather than acting unconsciously or operating on automatic pilot. When we see what we are doing, we see that we have choices. When we have choices, we become powerful. All of the Invitations in this book are designed to encourage you to become self-aware. In so doing, you will become free to make new choices and create new experiences.

Although my goal is not for you to believe me simply because "I say so," neither is it for you to discard what I say merely because it's a new way for you to think about things. Rather, I invite you to process the information and see if it makes sense to you. I invite you to try it. Experiment with it. Explore it. Practice it. Put it to the test. If even one skill or concept speaks to you and you make it your own through applying it, you will transform your relationships and your life.

PART ONE

THE MYTHOLOGY OF LOVE

Nonsense is that which does not fit into the prearranged patterns,
which we have superimposed on reality....
Nonsense is nonsense only when we have not yet found
that point of view from which it makes sense.
— GARY ZUKAV

The information in Part One is meant to help you make sense of the things you may have thought, felt, or experienced in the realm of relationships—possibly repeatedly—but perhaps did not understand.

The first step in learning how to bring about lasting change in your relationships is recognizing the beliefs that are impacting your current choices. In order to get where you want to go, you must know where you are right now.

1 Eros: The God of Love

If thou wingest thine arrows, Eros,
at once upon two hearts, thou art a god;
but not if thou piercest one only.

— UNKNOWN

Greek mythology always catches me a bit off guard. In my mind, gods and goddesses should be completely free from what I consider the very human characteristics of jealousy, revenge, anger, and manipulation. I want the gods to be role models of what works in the arena of love and relationships. But the Greek gods quite often personify some of our worst traits. They betray loved ones, seek revenge, or sentence people to a lifetime of misery. They cheat on their spouses, have sexual relations with animals, and are deceptive and manipulative.

It makes me wonder if humans were made in the "image and likeness of" these gods—or the other way around.

Eros, in Greek mythology, is the god of love. In Roman mythology, he is known as Cupid—a younger version of the same being. Both are depicted with wings, a bow and arrow, and often a torch. In some theories, Eros's mission was to spur procreation because it was believed that *eros* was one of the first powers in the universe, representing "the force of attraction and harmony that spurred all of creation."

While his beginning varies a bit from story to story, what remains a constant in all the tales of Eros is that he is the one who lights the flame of love or lust in the hearts of the gods and humans—or destroys it.

It is said that Eros carries a bow and quiver containing two types of arrows, one made with dove feathers and a golden point that arouses love and desire, and the other made with owl feathers and a lead point that causes indifference and apathy. As the mythology goes, once shot by Eros, you will find yourself hopelessly in love—or hopelessly apathetic, depending on which arrow he shot you with. He is also a bit of a prankster, often shooting only one person with the love arrow, or shooting the other with the arrow of apathy at some point in the relationship.

Unfortunately, this all leaves you—the dear lover—quite powerless and a potential victim of the wily and mischievous ways of Eros. Isn't this often the way we feel when it comes to love—as if we really have no control over our emotions and attractions?

The EROS Equation will give you a simple formula that serves as the antidote to the arrows of apathy, jealousy, rage, and manipulation. It will reveal a path that leads to love, harmony, and true intimacy in all of your relationships.

When we are equipped with the EROS Equation, we become immune to the "arrows" shot at us. Instead, we come to realize that we, the humans, can determine whether we are loving or apathetic, joyful or distressed, resistant or accepting. We realize that we are armed with the power of choice. This power serves as both a shield from the cunning ways of Eros and a tool we can use to govern our own love lives.

 **THE INVITATION** | *Explore Your Superpowers*

I invite you to explore the possibility that you are powerful. Human beings are blessed with "superpowers" that we rarely recognize. The power to choose, to see solutions, to think creatively, to use intuition, to access universal wisdom, to have compassion, and to solve problems should not be underestimated. These abilities may not be well exercised, or we may not even know we have them, but with a little awareness and training we can learn to harness them and put them to good use.

In the upcoming chapters, you will discover how to access and apply these abilities. For now consider the following: What are your superpowers? Are you creative? Intuitive? Intellectual? Able to forgive? Discerning? Perceptive? Emotional? Decisive? Resilient? Flexible? What are your personal abilities? When do you exercise them? And which of them would you like to develop?

It may be easier for you to identify your "super powers" if you think about something you have been successful at or something you have achieved. Then consider the skills and abilities that you had to utilize to reach that level of success. This could even be a relationship or friendship that was rewarding. Which qualities did you draw upon to make the friendship thrive? Sometimes we take our abilities for granted and dismiss them too easily. Look again. If you look deeper you will find your natural—or intentionally developed—strengths.

2 *Our Personal Mythology*

Something has got to hold it together.
I'm saying my prayers to Elmer,
the Greek god of glue.
— TOM ROBBINS

This is not a book about ancient mythology; it is a book about love and relationships, which, ironically, are full of mythology—our own personal mythologies. So bear with me if you are chomping at the bit to get to the part about relationships, because the topic of mythology is actually very relevant to what people do. It is undoubtedly relevant to what *you do* in relationships. Your job at this point is simply to begin to notice what you think and believe, and how those thoughts impact you and your choices. My job is to show you how you can change your mythology and transform your relationships, giving them not only a happy ending but a happy all-the-way-along.

When we stop to ponder what purposes mythology serves, a few come to mind. Virtually every culture has some form of mythology, which is essentially an ancient story that is often fictional and fanciful. Some mythology may be rooted in reality, but in the retelling through the ages the narrative becomes exaggerated and the characters become bigger, stronger, more inhuman—and sometimes more inhumane. This is akin to how prejudice develops. One or more people from a certain culture, race, religion, sexual orientation, age group, or gender behave a certain way, and in the repeating of the story that quality is assigned to every person in the group. So we end up with generalized beliefs like "All women are…," or "Men only want…." These beliefs become a part of our personal mythology and influence our choices and behaviors. Maybe it doesn't make a lot of sense, but it's what we humans do.

In many cases, mythologies develop from people's need to make sense of things we do not understand. When we don't understand what lightning is, it makes sense to create a story for our frightened children about a god who wields lightning bolts. And since human beings tend to take things personally, it follows that we would determine that everything from drought to flooding, feast to famine, love to hate are being imposed on us by some external source—for example, the arrows of Eros. Often, we personalize events to imply punishment or reward for deeds bad or good. My best guess is that this is our way of externalizing our conscience. When we feel guilty, "bad things" become punishment. When we are pleased with ourselves, "good things" become rewards. When bad things happen to good people, it doesn't make any sense under this belief system, so our ancestors created powerful—and sometimes evil—beings who rule over everything and who wreak havoc in human lives.

So mythology is how people find meaning in what they don't understand. And that is exactly what we do in relationships. The myth of Eros was undoubtedly an attempt to make sense of intense (and often unreasonable) desire, feelings of lack of control over our choices, and the fact that love sometimes fades. Clearly, humans who seem to have no say in the course of their passions have simply been shot with arrows.

When I first met my husband I felt as if I had been shot with the arrow of love and desire. A few years later, as you will read in Part Four, for no apparent reason I felt like I'd been shot with the arrow of apathy. At the time I felt completely powerless over the situation and thought my marriage was over. Then I employed the EROS Equation, reclaiming my "response-ability," and everything turned around. That is what I want to empower you to do.

♥THE INVITATION | Identify Your Mythology

Begin thinking about and identifying your personal mythology. Your personal mythology isn't limited to negative beliefs or falsehoods; it may simply be the way you make sense of your life, your expectations, or even others' behavior. What beliefs have you taken on about love and relationships? What beliefs have you taken on about your role in love and relationships? What generalizations (positive or negative) have you cast upon all men or all women due to what a few have done?

Even our definitions are part of our personal mythology. What are your beliefs about what "marriage" means? Sex? Commitment? Family? Who do you blame or credit outside of yourself for your reality? What do you believe about who you are, why you are here, and whether you matter? Take a moment to recognize that you actually do have a mythology all your own, one that may have started in truth but grew in the retelling into a set of beliefs that either limit you or provide constructive guidance.

3 Making Meaning

As small children we develop a process of interpreting the things we see and hear. This is how our critical-thinking skills begin to develop, how we start "connecting the dots" and making sense of our surroundings. The problem is that we have a fairly limited range of information, so the conclusions we draw are not always accurate. In addition, since we tend to take things very personally starting at a young age, we absorb information as a means of figuring out who we are and what our place is in the world and in the lives of those we love. In essence, we think that what happens outside of us means something about who we are. And since we don't know how to interpret events, we invent meanings that become part of our personal mythology.

Let me give you an example. I have a young friend who texts me, often when my phone is silenced because I'm in a meeting or with a client. If I don't immediately reply, she continues sending texts, each one more anxious in tone than the last, until finally she sends one that says something like, "I knew you never loved me and that I don't matter to you. Everyone else is more important than I am. I never want to talk to you again." She has started "making meaning" from my actions (or, in this case, my lack of action). Since she doesn't have the complete information—that I'm with a client or otherwise unavailable—her young mind tries to make sense of why I am not responding to her. Unfortunately, we often learn at a very young age to draw the worst possible conclusions, usually based in fear, and often in familial and societal training. My friend in this example made up a story about why she hadn't heard back from me, and it became a belief, part of her personal mythology.

Such actions seem absurd to us when we watch someone else do them, especially when we know the truth about why I didn't respond. As I said, my friend is quite young. Indeed, I wish this process of making meaning were limited to inexperienced kids, but it's not. Let's look at other ways in which making meaning creates havoc in our relationships. These may hit closer to home.

Have you ever sent an important e-mail or text to someone you love, only to get no response? If so, did you find yourself making up a story about how the other person was ignoring you or didn't care? Of course, there are myriad other possible reasons why you didn't hear back from them, including that the e-mail never arrived or went into a spam folder, or that they didn't see your text.

Now that many of us have the ability to read e-mail on our cell phones but much less ability to respond nimbly via "thumb typing," maybe we see an important, heartfelt e-mail and think, *This is too important to reply to on the run. I'll wait until I get to my computer so I can send a more thoughtful response*. By the time we get home, perhaps hundreds more e-mails have arrived, distracting us from our intention to reply to the original e-mail right away, and the sender concludes that they must not matter to us. Sound familiar?

Or how about when your sweetheart is supposed to be home at 6:00 PM and isn't? Do you make meaning that he or she has been in an accident? Or having an affair? That he or she doesn't really care about you or respect you? Do you work yourself into a frenzy until your partner gets home, and then thrust your personal mythology upon them as if it were the truth?

Imagine you are getting ready to go out to dinner and you notice your partner looking you over. Not knowing what the look implies, you may make meaning that draws any number of self-defeating conclusions. *He doesn't like what I am wearing. She thinks I am too fat. He thinks this outfit is too sexy. He thinks it isn't sexy enough. She thinks I'm too casual. He thinks I wore this last time we went out.* In essence, you project onto your partner whatever you may be thinking about yourself—none of which may be true for him or her. Then you may cast your personal mythology onto your partner and get angry, defensive, or short for reasons that are totally unknown to the other person. Chances are they were just thinking, *She has her shoes, her keys, her purse, she is ready to go*. Or better yet, *She looks great*. After all, if we are just making up what the other is thinking without truly knowing, we may as well make up something good, right?

A while ago a funny e-mail was circulating that exemplified this issue. A couple was driving down the road and she announced, "Hey, today is our six-month anniversary!" To which he replied, "Hey, yeah, it is! Wow!" Then you got to peer into their heads to see what they were thinking. His next thoughts were, *Wow. Six months! Whoa, wasn't that about when I last got the oil changed in the car? Could it really have been six months? I better get on it and get the oil changed!* Meanwhile, she is making meaning of his silence, thinking, *He isn't saying anything. He is thinking he can't believe we made it this long. He doesn't want to continue! He is trying to figure out how to break up with me!* She blurts out, "Okay, let's just break up!" to a very bewildered boyfriend who can't figure out how they went from celebrating their anniversary to breaking up during a five-minute drive. An arrow was shot into the heart of the relationship straight from her personal mythology.

The main problem with beliefs is that the minute we turn a thought or a possible meaning into a belief, we stop inquiring. Remember, just because you believe something doesn't mean it's true, and just because you don't believe something doesn't mean it isn't true. However, when you deeply believe something, you may behave in a way that will eventually make it true. So take a careful look at your beliefs to see if they are truly serving you.

 ## Question Your Beliefs

I invite you to take a look at how you make meaning out of events and out of others' behavior and words. Next, do some self-inquiry about the truth of your thoughts, or explore the matter with your partner. Take another look to see if the meaning you made is actually true. Are you sure? How do you behave and how do you feel on account of the meaning you've made? How does your personal mythology or belief system impact the way you make meaning?

How do your beliefs impact your relationships? What beliefs have you taken on about relationships, men, women, love, your abilities, your worthiness? Are any of them actually true? Are you sure? Consider: If you are just making up a story anyhow, how can you make up a story that makes you feel good instead of bad?

PART TWO

THE COMMON DENOMINATOR:
YOU

There are two basic motivating forces: fear and love.
When we are afraid, we pull back from life. When we are in love,
we open to all that life has to offer with passion, excitement, and
acceptance. We need to learn to love ourselves first, in all our glory
and our imperfections. If we cannot love ourselves, we cannot fully
open to our ability to love others or our potential to create.
— JOHN LENNON

Our relationship with self is the foundation of all our other relationships. The following chapters will deepen your understanding of who you are and how your self-esteem impacts your relationships—and vice versa.

This understanding will help you open the door to your heart and access the wealth of wisdom, intuition, and creativity that dwells there. These resources will make you powerful in the realm of relationships and joyful in life.

4 Who You Really Are

> *Only the truth of who you are,*
> *if realized, will set you free.*
> — ECKHART TOLLE

In a temple in Bangkok is the world's largest solid-gold Buddha statue. At one time it was housed in a temple in Ayutthaya. It is believed that in the 1700s, the monks there heard that Burmese soldiers were heading their way, raiding communities and stealing everything of value. Unable to hide or move the five-and-a-half-ton, ten-foot-tall statue, they decided to conceal it by plastering it over with clay. Their plan worked well in that the invaders didn't recognize the statue as anything of value; however, the town was destroyed, and all the people who knew the true nature of the statue were killed. In the 1950s, when the "clay" Buddha was being moved to a new location, a strap broke and a piece of the plaster chipped off. Horrified at first that they had damaged the ancient artifact, the movers then discovered the stunning golden statue inside.

I share this true story because it is my observation that we humans are exactly like the statue.

At our core, we are spirits of love. We come together in relationship to love and be loved. That is the mission of the spirit.

When we are authentic, love is not something that has to be manipulated or that we have to try to do. It is just what is. The ocean doesn't have to try to be wet, a puppy doesn't have to try to be cute, and we do not have to try to love or be loved. Love is our True Nature.

As we grow up, our authentic, brilliant True Nature gets covered over by protective beliefs, mythologies, meanings, and behaviors. We forget the truth of who we are and begin to think that the false beliefs and behaviors that we deploy for protection are our true selves. The problem is that, in the realm of love, emotional armor, false beliefs, and manipulative behaviors are not the ingredients for great relationships.

We hear a lot of talk about "being authentic" and "our true essence" and "being transparent" and "who we really are," but most of us are a little confused about exactly what that essence is and what it has to do with our relationships.

It is my experience that we are, in our True Nature, spiritual, esteemed beings: intuitive, wise, compassionate, caring, accepting, loving, powerful, creative, discerning. These are the very ingredients required to build loving, sustainable relationships. We have simply forgotten how to access them effortlessly and easily. All we need is to be reminded how to uncover these latent aspects of ourselves and share them with others. There is nothing more attractive.

Our True Nature, or "higher self," operates from love, trust, faith, wisdom, creativity, and intuition. Our True Nature is unafraid, knowing that everything is an opportunity to grow and learn and that with a little time and perspective, we will come to understand the value of our circumstances. When we are authentic, we do not have to manipulate to be loved and loving. Love just exists.

Consider the positive qualities of small children before they have been "contaminated" by the world. They are inherently playful, funny, creative, honest, imaginative, curious, wonder-filled, loving, joyful, enthusiastic, and adventurous. They are authentic and in the moment with their emotions; they laugh when they are happy, cry when they are sad, and forget about whatever it was that upset them as soon as it is fixed or something new happens. They are natural learners, wanting to know what everything is called and how it works. They are creative and imaginative, able to build a magnificent fort out of a few blankets and chairs. Children are able to take compliments, aware of their own worth and confident that the compliments are true. Small children get along with others regardless of race, religion, gender, or handicaps, as they haven't yet learned to judge. They are forgiving, as living in the present moment doesn't allow them to hold a grudge. They are closely aligned with their esteemed self because they haven't yet had life experiences that have separated their ego from their spirit in an attempt at self-protection. Small children know their divine essence. All they do is an authentic expression of who they are.

Keep in mind that this is true not only of the children outside of you, but also of the child inside of you. You were like this as a child, too. These childlike qualities are an expression of your soul. They represent "who you really are."

However, somewhere along the way we start to make meaning about ourselves out of events that happen and things people say to us. What may have started out as a "you statement" ("you're stupid" or "you're not good enough") or an event we didn't understand turned into an "I statement" ("I'm stupid" or "I'm not good enough"). These painfully negative beliefs often become "who we think we are." In an effort to protect us from this pain, the egoic mind begins to develop.

Because these beliefs are painful and unattractive, we eventually hide them from the world and put on a false exterior to protect ourselves. The protective façade becomes "who we want everyone to think we are" and can take many forms, such as an effort to be perfect, or to have expensive toys represent us. Or it may take the form of obliviousness ("I don't know") or apathy ("I don't care"). To the ego, not trying, or destroying the game, beats losing. Even a misplaced smile or incongruent laughter or humor can serve as the protective layer. These attempts to keep people from hurting us also keep people (and ourselves) from seeing the truth of who we are.

Over time, we forget that our authentic, "golden" center—our pure, childlike qualities—are even there, and we begin to believe instead that we are the clay, the protective layer. The problem is that while the "clay" may keep out the pain and keep others from recognizing us, it also keeps out the love and keeps others from connecting with us. This unconscious reality definitely impacts our relationships. I explain this protective process much more fully in Part Three, "Ego Battleships vs. Real-ationships."

The good news is that our authentic qualities never go away; access to them just gets blocked. With a little concerted effort, we can retrieve all these magnificent attributes. With a little self-discovery, a little understanding, a few great tools, and a little practice, you can unlock the door to your heart—often with one simple breath.

THE
INVITATION   Look a Little Deeper

See if you can find evidence that what I am saying is true. Examine your "clay" exterior. Explore the behaviors and pretenses you have adopted for protection and to manipulate others to love you. Do you smile or laugh when you don't mean it? Do you act like you don't care when you do? Do you have to make everything perfect so people don't see your faults? Do you keep expensive, shiny things around you to impress others? Do you use humor to deflect intimacy? Do you say, "I don't know" to avoid being wrong? Do you act like you are right even when you aren't sure? Do you use sexuality to attract attention?

This invitation is not to judge yourself. We all have defense mechanisms that served us well before we were mature enough to protect ourselves more appropriately. This is simply an invitation to discover what you do. When you know what you do, when you catch yourself doing it, you have the ability to decide whether it is serving you or not. And you begin to recognize that you are also creating the consequences of what you do.

Next, look even deeper to see if you can identify your good qualities. What are the positive traits that describe you? What are your strengths, gifts, talents, and abilities?

When you begin to identify and focus on your good qualities, you will begin to hear others recognizing them as well—not the other way around. When you acknowledge and honor your goodness, you will be able to hear the kind words of others (who may have been honoring you all along without your awareness). When you know who you really are, you will make wiser choices that reflect that knowing. It all starts with taking a deeper look. What do you like, love, admire, or appreciate about yourself?

5 *The Role of Self-Esteem in Relationships*

> *Because one believes in oneself, one doesn't try to convince others. Because one is content with oneself, one doesn't need others' approval. Because one accepts oneself, the whole world accepts him or her.*
> — LAO TZU

In order to explain what happens to love between two people, we need to begin by understanding what happens to self-love—or self-esteem. Since you are the primary ingredient—and the common denominator—in all of your relationships, you will see the definite correlation between the strength of your self-esteem and the health of your relationships. Understanding the dynamics of self-esteem—what happens to it as we grow up, and how to put it back on the right path—not only will help you feel better about yourself, which will certainly contribute to good relationships, but also will assist you in enhancing the self-esteem of the people you love most: your family, sweetheart, and children.

Let's clear up some serious misconceptions about self-esteem.

We have mistakenly thought that ego or conceit and self-esteem are the same thing, and they are not. Self-esteem is based on our inherent worth and strength as human beings—our soul essence. Ego is based on our minds—what we think—not on who we are at our core. Ego pushes people away while self-esteem attracts them. To use the example from the last chapter, ego is like the clay while self-esteem is the solid-gold Buddha inside.

By the nature of our common language on the subject, we have created the misunderstanding that self-esteem is "high" or "low." Self-esteem is referred to here as "high" and "low" simply for convenience, but we don't really have high or low levels of self-esteem. Our True Nature is naturally highly esteemed, and we have either easy access or blocked access to it. The same is true for love. Love doesn't go away, it just gets blocked.

We have mistakenly thought that once we have achieved healthy self-esteem, it is ours for good. In actuality, self-esteem, much like physical fitness, has to be continuously and consciously maintained. But once healthy self-esteem has been achieved, the "lows" don't go as deep and a pathway back out of the depths has been forged so you don't stay down as long. Relationships also require this ongoing maintenance and mindfulness.

There is a mistaken belief that self-esteem is "global," meaning that if someone has self-esteem in one area of their life, they have it in all areas. In reality, someone can feel good about his or her performance at work and terrible about his or her relationships at home. Someone can have high self-esteem in regard to their productivity or creativity and low self-esteem around their body image.

We have greatly underestimated the impact of self-esteem on our relationships by mistakenly thinking that the health of our self-esteem impacts only how we feel about ourselves. In fact, our self-esteem also impacts our ability to feel loved by others, to feel worthy of the love of others, and to share our love with others. If we do not love ourselves, we cannot fully believe that others love us. If we do not feel worthy of love, we will sabotage our relationships to prove that we were right about our lack of worthiness. If we do not feel love within us, we are not able to share our love with others. If we cannot love ourselves unconditionally, forgive ourselves for our mistakes, and experience joy and happiness on a daily basis, we cannot love others unconditionally, forgive them when necessary, and accept their forgiveness. When we love ourselves, we are fully able to share our joy and happiness with others.

Self-esteem is not a matter of whether you see the glass half empty or half full. Rather, it is about whether you know how to fill it back up. I define self-esteem as "knowing our True Nature and living in alignment with it." When we know our authentic selves, we can pick ourselves up when the world deals us a blow, find the blessing in any situation, and move inward, onward, and upward.

It has almost become a cliché to state that we must love ourselves in order to be loved and loving, but it is ultimately the truth and deserves repeating. In the following chapters you will begin to see how to access love and what blocks love, not only with others but also for yourself. The Essential Life and Love Skills in Part Six are great steps for turning your self-esteem around as well as turning your love life with others around. It is imperative that we begin to be mindful of what we say to ourselves and how we treat ourselves so that we become clear about how we will allow others to treat us.

You will discover in Part Three that a huge amount of our self-esteem issues stems from misinterpreting the ego's self-talk. As we begin to understand the role of this inner voice that is often fraught with negativity, we will learn how to translate its message into something helpful rather than hurtful.

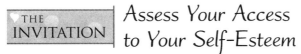 **Assess Your Access to Your Self-Esteem**

After you read this, I invite you to close your eyes and imagine that you are looking at your own mirrored image, into your own eyes. While your real eyes are closed, imagine saying into the eyes

of your mirrored image, "I love you and accept you just the way you are." Then watch your how your imagined mirrored image responds and how you feel. When you are done, open your eyes.

When I ask people to do this, some say they felt happy and good telling themselves they loved themselves. Some say they are aware they don't say it enough. Others, like me the first time I did it, are moved to tears over how uncomfortable and untrue it feels. My mirrored image rolled her eyes and said sarcastically, "Yeah, sure you do." If this describes you, your discomfort is merely a light that is shining on where the work needs to be done.

If the exercise felt good, do it some more, but use a real mirror. If it didn't feel good, do it some more using a real mirror. I invite you to do the "mirror exercise" every morning and every night in a real mirror. Look into your own eyes, breathe, and tell yourself what you like, love, admire, or appreciate about yourself. Feel free to recap the successes of your day; acknowledge your strengths, efforts, and even your baby steps. Keep breathing, hold the eye contact, and tell yourself, "I love you." If that is too much of a stretch, start with "I like you," or "I appreciate you." It is okay to fall in love slowly—with others or yourself.

Eventually, you will begin to replace the automatic, unconscious negative self-talk with a more loving, supportive commentary. As this happens, you will be on your own team and moving in the direction of your success, instead of acting as your own opposition.

6 The Key to Your Heart

> The best and most beautiful things in the
> world cannot be seen or even touched—
> they must be felt with the heart.
>
> — HELEN KELLER

My personal philosophy is that all around us and within us is a never-ending source of love that we can access at any time. There doesn't necessarily have to be an object of our affection in order for us to feel love. Our souls are love. Our natural state is love. What happens to most of us, though, is that we close our hearts, which is like closing a door so that the love cannot stream in—or out—freely. We do this for protection, but it becomes the very obstacle to what we want. It is like the story in Chapter 4. We forget that we are the "golden Buddha" and believe we are the clay.

We say, "You hold the key to my heart" when someone is able— through their words or touch or smile or chemistry—to help us unlock the door. The love of our soul then floods us, filling our being. The person who helps us to open our heart becomes the object of that love out of our gratefulness to them for helping us experience our soul's capacity.

Relationships can be such a beautiful flow of love between two open hearts. We help someone to feel the love within them; they help us to feel the love within us; we share our love with each other. Our love runs over and spills onto everything around us. We become different. When we are in love with someone, we feel love for everything more easily. The access is open.

The sad thing is that we often credit the other person entirely for the way we feel, when we actually have had that capacity for love all along. The problem with giving the credit away is that, if the person leaves us, we think we no longer have the key, or the access to that source. We close the door to our heart and feel cut off from love. We so often give our power away, thinking that someone else holds the only set of keys, leaving ourselves feeling empty or powerless without him or her.

The Internet has widened our circle of friendships through online dating and social networking. It provides a perfect example of the way we externalize our experience. When we encounter someone online whom we don't actually know, and they say to us loving, kind, comforting, or romantic things, we begin to open the door to our hearts and let our love flow. It is easy to feel love bubbling to the surface as we read about walking on the beach together hand-in-hand and to believe it's the other person who is causing us to feel love—even though we haven't met them. Then, if we meet him or her in person and feel nothing, we blame them for the loss.

We do the same thing in our face-to-face relationships. When our date or sweetheart behaves a certain way, we feel loved and loving. When they don't, we don't. We turn our hearts over to others on a silver platter, as if surrendering our capability to love and be loved to Eros and his arrows. We begin to think that people and circumstances outside of ourselves are in control of our feelings of love.

Recognizing that it wasn't the other person who caused your feelings of love—but rather that you merely accessed your own source of love—can help you recognize that the love didn't go away when that person left or disappointed you. You just closed the door again. The other person never held the key in the first place; he or she just activated your choice to love.

Love is an inside job. It isn't like someone actually hands us something we get to hold and touch. Love isn't something we possess; it's something we access.

We want to blame others for the lack of love in our lives, but the irony is that it is possible to love someone who doesn't love you in return, and most of us have. Conversely, someone could love you with all of his or her heart, and you still might not feel loved. Or someone may not even know you exist, and you could feel full of love for them. The other person's participation is not required for us to feel love. The love is within us. It is who we are; other people just help us retrieve it.

The source of our love is not outside of us. Love exists regardless of what other people do, and it is our job to learn how to access it no matter what they do. This is how we become powerful in the realm of relationships.

What I am saying is true for both the love you give and the love you receive. Love exists within you, totally independently of the object of your love (or the absence of someone to share that love with). Love has little to do with the proximity or even the existence of the other person. When you love someone and they die, the love remains. Even when we break up with someone, love doesn't always go away. We just block its flow.

It is helpful to know that we can open the door to our heart ourselves. We can love life, we can love nature, we can love ourselves, we can love God, and we can love love. By raising our self-esteem and accessing the well of love within, we can live in alignment with our souls—in love all the time. By doing so we will have much more love to share with others. Perhaps even more important, we will not cling to our mates like energy vampires, in search of love that they really can't give us. We have to feel love within.

When two people come together who are already feeling love—for themselves and for life—they have love to share and don't need the other person to feel complete. Being together simply amplifies the joy.

This is important to recognize because it allows us to make life a treasure hunt for the multitude of keys that can open our heart, helping us to be more loving and to feel more love throughout our lives—regardless of what the people around us choose to do. This allows our love to be experienced as an authentic, independent reality, all the time.

 *Find Love Within*

Start by aiming to experience the feeling of love—regardless of the presence or absence of a partner. To do this, make a "Love List." List everything you love, such as memories, people, tastes, colors, movies, books, and (importantly) aspects of yourself. Think of the things that help you feel the love that is already within you and for which you are grateful. Once your list is finished, read through it, and pause at each item to hold a vision of it in your mind's eye. For instance, maybe you put "sunsets" on your list. Sit quietly, envision a memorable sunset, and see if you can feel the love inside you. Continue with each item on your list. Consciously let your love grow, and begin to recognize what it feels like. Then, throughout your day, look for things to love and to be joyful about—even little things, like finding a parking spot in a crowded lot, receiving a kind smile from a stranger, spotting a flower growing through a

crack in the cement. Feel free to add items to your list as you discover them. Notice what love and appreciation feel like, and begin to allow that feeling to flow through you all the time.

Equally, notice when you disallow the feeling of love. In those moments, guaranteed, your ego is at work. You will block the flow of love when you are judging others or yourself, when you are trying to control others, or when you are trying to gain their approval. You will block the flow of love when you are inauthentic (in other words, dishonest or withholding the truth). Simply notice when you are blocking love. Then take a deep breath—or two, or three, or four—and see if you can realign with the feeling of love that you have been developing. Surround yourself with things that help you feel love—nature, beauty, kittens, puppies, music, creativity—and practice seeing if you can begin to hold that feeling all the time, regardless of an external influence.

When you are in a relationship, enjoy the power and beauty of two people feeling the love within at the same time and sharing it with each other—rather than getting it from each other. This is, indeed, a beautiful thing.

PART THREE

EGO BATTLESHIPS
VS. REAL-ATIONSHIPS

The Ego is a veil between humans and God.
— RUMI

We all have access to the resources we need to make love and relationships work. Unfortunately, few if any of us have been taught how to unlock the door to those resources and let the love flow. Consequently, our relationships have more closely resembled a power struggle than a sharing of the heart.

The following chapters will reveal to you, perhaps for the first time, the obstacles to love and how to overcome them in order to experience a real-ationship.

7 The Number-One Obstacle in Relationships

> *The ego relies on the familiar. It is reluctant to experience the unknown, which is the very essence of life.*
>
> — DEEPAK CHOPRA

Why do our relationships, once full of love, go astray? Because of our egos. Ego is the number-one obstacle to relationships—but it doesn't mean to be.

In our society, the ego has gotten a bad rap. And, in truth, the ego can be responsible for some pretty nasty behaviors. However, I would like to paint a different picture of the ego—and its motive. When we understand the nature of the ego, we can work with it instead of against it and harness its power to help us instead of hurt us.

The sole motive of the ego is to protect us at all costs, even if the cost is the loss of the very joy and love we seek.

Imagine that the ego is like an overprotective parent who says and does all the wrong things in an effort to keep you safe. An overprotective parent may stop you from going outside so you don't get hurt, may say mean and controlling things to try to keep you from venturing out, or may try to stop you from dating so you don't suffer a breakup or commit yourself to the wrong person. He or she may even say unkind things to manipulate you to stay in the safety of your room—telling you, for example, that you aren't smart or capable enough to do what you want to do. While it may look, sound, or feel like the parent doesn't care about you, chances are he or she is really trying to protect you and simply doesn't know how (perhaps because of his or her own unresolved ego issues—but that's another topic). The ego operates in exactly the same way.

The ego, through beliefs and the "self-talk babble" you hear in your head, may sound like it hates you, thinks horrible things about you, doesn't trust you or anyone else, and believes that you are unworthy of love. The truth, though, is that your ego-mind wants you to be safe from harm. Driven by its desire to protect you, it gets involved in all you do (if you let it), including your love life.

The ego—being overprotective—resorts to using fear, jealousy, possessiveness, manipulation, anger, apathy, withdrawal, revenge, and hurt in an effort to keep you safe and to make sure your needs are met. As I'm sure you can imagine, however, these behaviors don't work well in the realm of love, even though almost everyone unconsciously resorts to them, at least occasionally.

Ego is especially triggered into action when some kind of commitment has been made—like dating exclusively, introducing sex into the relationship, agreeing to be monogamous, moving in together, deciding to get married, or having children. These are all big ego triggers. We have all known couples who were together for years before getting married, and then immediately after the wedding their relationship began to fall apart. This is likely because the new level of commitment activated their egos. Instead of allowing them to love each other naturally and by choice, their egos suddenly began thinking that loving is something it *had* to do. As a result, the partners resorted to new methods of getting their needs met—methods that simply don't work.

When we try to silence or ignore the voice of the ego, it gets louder and nastier because it doesn't feel heard. Let's return to the analogy of the overprotective parent. Say you were a teenager and asked your overprotective parent for the keys to the car. Your parent, worried for your well-being and trying to protect you, lists the fear-based reasons not to give you the keys: "No. I am afraid you will get in an accident. Your friends will distract you. You might talk on your phone while driving. You could drive drunk and kill yourself." He or she may even belittle your skills. If, in response, you dismiss or ignore what your parent said and ask for the keys again, chances are your parent will feel that none of his or her concerns were heard or honored. Your parent repeats what he or she said earlier, but this time more loudly and possibly more dysfunctionally, demeaning your abilities and undermining your confidence. "You don't have enough experience driving—you won't know what to do. You aren't a good enough driver." If, however, instead of ignoring what your parent said the first time, you listen carefully, let your parent know that you heard their concerns and present a strategy for avoiding problems, he or she will probably lighten up and may even give you the keys. When the parent believes that you have a strategy for protection in place, they begin to trust you.

The ego is exactly like that. The "self-talk" of your ego will try to stop you and may paint the worst-case scenario, demeaning and belittling you to try to keep you safe. In the realm of love this may sound like some variation of "You are not good enough. You don't deserve love. He or she is going to cheat on you with someone thinner, taller, younger, richer, prettier, more handsome. Love doesn't last. He or she doesn't really love you. You shouldn't trust him or her."

If you simply take what the ego says at face value and believe it, the result will be depression, fear, and stagnancy. You may give up or not even try for whatever it was you wanted.

If, however, you listen with your heart instead of your head and think about the real message behind the words of your ego, you will be able to make a different meaning. You will hear the concern in your ego's self-talk and utilize your skills to strategize a healthier approach to the situation. What the ego really means is, *I want the best for you. I want you to be safe*. However, it has no skills for communicating this, so it resorts to manipulating you.

A funny instance of the need to listen to the message behind the ego's self-talk (i.e., to interpret the ego) happened to me when I was making a presentation on self-esteem. I was explaining the concept of self-talk when I heard my own ego say, *You are so boring. Look at that man in the front row; he is falling asleep.* If I'd listened to the statement solely at its face value, the belief that I was boring could have caused me to "flatline" on the stage and completely fail. However, knowing that the self-talk voice of ego was trying to protect me, I realized that the meaning it was making out of the situation may or may not have been true. So I looked around for evidence. No one else was sleeping. I then considered other possible meanings. Perhaps the man was from a different time zone or wasn't feeling well and his sleepiness had nothing to do with me. Perhaps he thought my talk was so engaging he didn't want to leave even though he was tired. I considered all the options and determined that a better course of action than simply believing the negative self-talk was to use it to my advantage. I invited everyone to stand up and do an exercise that raised the energy in the room. Rather than crumbling under the weight of my self-talk, I had to laugh at the way the ego works and appreciate that it was trying to help me. After all, the irony of negative self-talk during a presentation on self-esteem is a bit amusing.

 *Develop an Ego Interpreter*

What has your ego stopped you from doing or caused you to do in an effort to protect you? What does your self-talk tell you? See if you can listen to the voice of ego without simply believing it. Can you see the true motive of protection at work? Can you identify other methods or strategies of protection that are more in alignment with what you want to create?

8 The Ego Magnet

As we discussed in Chapter 4, "Who We Really Are,"
our authentic selves come together in relationship to love and be
loved. However, the ego gets ahold of that concept, and although
it wants to help—it wants to make sure you give and receive love—
it doesn't know how.

The ego doesn't realize that if it were to stay out of the way,
the spirit is fully capable of loving and being loved. Instead, the
ego thinks, *I have to love and have to be loved.* Then it goes to great
effort to make sure that happens.

The ego thinks, *I could love so-and-so if they would only make a certain amount of money/make love the way I want/eat the right foods/clean
house/quit smoking/quit drinking/weigh a certain amount.* It comes up
with a long list of things the other person could do differently

to deserve your love. The natural and authentic state of loving someone, through the filter of ego, turns into the need to control him or her.

On the flip side, in an effort to be sure you are loved, the ego thinks, *I can get so-and-so to love me if I dress the way they want me to/ keep the house clean/watch the movies they like/smile enough/have sex with him or her.* It comes up with a long list of behaviors we think we can employ to manipulate someone else into loving us. We think that if we just alter ourselves to be what the other person wants us to be, he or she will love us. Through the filter of ego, the natural essence of being loved turns into a need for approval.

Unfortunately, the behaviors that accompany these ego-needs actually become the very obstacles to loving and being loved. (I will explain the need for control and the need for approval more fully in the next couple of chapters.) It is my experience that the ego is just like a magnet with two polarized ends, one positive and one negative. If you put the same ends of two magnets together, the magnets repel each other. If you put opposite ends together, they attract each other. At one end of the ego magnet is a strong need for approval that is motivated by the need to be loved. At the other end of the ego magnet is a strong need to control that is motivated by the need to love.

We all have both ends of the "magnet," the ego-need for approval and the ego-need for control, but we tend to lead with one or the other. We flip back and forth depending on whom we are with or the circumstances we are facing, but we all tend to return to the "default setting" of one or the other in how we deal with our loved ones. When we approach a sweetheart or coworker with one magnetized end of our ego fully activated, we attract the opposite reaction from that person. The need for approval attracts control, and the need for control attracts approval-seeking. Two people vying for control duke it out, and two people with a need for approval repulse each other.

To put it another way, both the need for approval and the need for control are the clay covering up who we really are—which is a being who is capable of creating healthy, happy relationships.

When I was unconscious of this state of affairs, I led with my ego-need for approval as if I were holding up a giant magnetized puzzle piece on my forehead. I couldn't see it, but clearly others around me could feel it. All I saw was that my friends, my sweethearts, and my coworkers all appeared to be control freaks. I allowed myself to be molded into what others wanted, and I did what I thought would please them in an effort to get approval. If you had asked me, I would have blamed them for their controlling ways and for my choices. Now that I understand this dynamic, I can see that I evoked a controlling response from them because of the ego magnet I was presenting.

The goal is to find the point in the center where the magnetic pull of the ego is neutralized or in balance. I'll explain more about this sense of balance in Chapter 12, "Restoring Balance and Authenticity," but for now let's look more closely at each end of the ego-magnet so you more fully understand how it works.

♥ THE INVITATION | *Feel the Attraction*

Can you see which ego-need tends to rule you? If you experience a lot of self-doubt or often seek the acceptance of others, your need for approval is likely the end of the ego magnet you lead with in relationships. If you find yourself judging and critical of others, your need for control is likely the end of the magnet you lead with in relationships. Do you lead with one ego-need in some relationships and the opposite ego-need in others?

If you can't tell which you lead with, can you identify the magnets in those around you? Since we tend to attract individuals who present the opposite magnetic pull, noticing the orientation of the magnets in the people around us can help us see our own.

Remember, a need for approval is the ego's attempt to be loved, and a need for control is the ego's attempt to love. Yet both become the very obstacles to love. As you notice what you do, notice whether it is working to achieve the ultimate goal of love.

I invite you to simply notice, because until we know what we do, we cannot make choices to change it.

9 *The Need for Control*

> *People don't resist change.*
> *They resist being changed.*
> — PETER M. SENGE

When you find yourself feeling judgmental and critical of another, your need for control has been activated. Even if you don't say anything out loud, but simply judge in silence, your magnet is stimulated and the other person can feel it. Initially they may try to appease you in an attempt to get your approval, but eventually, when that seems impossible, the relationship will falter.

Remember, if we are authentic, love just exists; it isn't something we have to try to do or force. However, the ego, in a desperate attempt to protect and help us, wants to make sure we are both loved and loving, so it gets involved. Your soul's desire to love, through the filter of ego, becomes a need for control.

The ego thinks it would be a lot easier to love another if they would behave the way we wanted them to, and, as highlighted in the last chapter, it has a long list of demands. The challenge is that trying to meet all the expectations of the ego becomes a never-ending, unattainable quest.

If you, with a need for approval, clean the kitchen to satisfy your partner with a need for control, it won't work. Someone with a need for control will soon see something else on the list: "What about the bathroom, or the bedroom? Have you seen the laundry?" Trying to appease someone with a need for control is impossible, especially when we continue to evoke that quality in them with our magnetized need for approval.

I once worked with a woman who was stuck in her marriage. Her ego magnet presented with a need to control. She told me that her husband had given her a pair of diamond earrings, but she was angry that they weren't the ones she wanted and that he had given them to her several years later than she had requested them. When someone is immersed in the ego-need for control, nothing appeases them.

The other harsh reality is that "control" emanating from ego is a total illusion. We cannot sustain controlling another; they will eventually retaliate and do what they want—or they will recoil and emotionally "flatline." This may include doing exactly what you *don't* want them to do, just to spite your effort to control. You tell your kids they can't smoke, so they go behind a building to do it. You tell them they can't go out, so they sneak out through the window. Most egos don't like to be controlled, and they find ways to assert themselves, often behind your back. The arrows of revenge and passive-aggressiveness have been shot.

I know that some of you are thinking, *But I am the husband (or father or wife or mother or boss) and I have to be in control.* It is true that you need to have influence and authentic power. However, if you are leading from your ego rather than from that authentic power, your sweetheart (or child or colleague) will retaliate. You may discover them sabotaging you behind your back, showing up late, and getting away with as much as they possibly can. When you attempt to love, or lead, with your ego, you will meet resistance. When you lead with your authentic power you will have influence and your loved ones or colleagues will be more likely to work with you instead of against you.

Imagine walking into a room where you discovered a sleeping bear. You would move cautiously and quietly so as not to wake the bear, or you would exit the room as quickly as possible. If you awakened the bear it could be dangerous. If, on the other hand, you walked into a room and found a puppy, you would most likely take some time to love it up and then go about your business. In either case you would be aware of the animal, but in one case with fear and trepidation and in the other with happiness and pleasure.

When one or the other partner has activated his or her ego magnet, it is as if there were a bear in the room. Even if nothing is said or done (i.e., the bear is sleeping), the other partner has a heightened awareness of the danger, and their behavior is going to be different. By contrast, when we transcend our ego and realign with our authenticity, it changes the atmosphere.

 *Notice*

In what situations do feel a need for control? Who do you judge? Do you have to be right (or are you certain that you are)? Do you catch yourself finding fault with others, wishing they were different, thinking you know better than they do? Again, this is not an invitation to turn that judgment on yourself, only to observe what you do and when you do it.

Next, simply notice if the choice to judge others and to try to control them makes your relationships stronger or weaker. Notice whether those behaviors make you feel better and closer to each other or worse and farther away. Notice whether trying to control other people is actually working for you. Just notice.

If, once you have noticed, you decide to continue doing it anyhow, that is your choice. Just know that every choice comes with a consequence that you are also choosing. It is far better to be judgmental by choice than by unconscious habit. When we do so unconsciously, we end up blaming the people we judged for the consequence, rather than recognizing our choice and, thus, our responsibility.

10 The Need for Approval

> *Everything will line up perfectly when knowing and living the truth become more important than looking good.*
>
> — ALAN COHEN

When you find yourself full of self-doubt, lacking confidence, questioning your actions and decisions, or seeking compliments or confirmation from others, there is a good chance your magnet has turned the other way around. These are the signs and symptoms of the need for approval.

The need for approval afflicts all of us some of the time, and some of us all of the time. The challenge with a strong need for approval is that we veer away from who we really are and try to be who we think the other person wants us to be. The more we behave the way we think they want us to (or the way they actually want us to), the farther we wander from our authentic, "golden" self. The problems with this inauthenticity are numerous, especially when we try to please multiple people who have conflicting expectations.

First, we are putting on a façade, a clay exterior, and sometimes it works so well that we forget we are faking it. Then, when the object of our desire admires the façade or tells us they love us when we are being inauthentic, we don't believe them. On some level, we know they are loving who we pretend to be, not the real deal. They are loving the clay, not the gold. When someone tells us something we don't believe, we think they must be lying. This is no different.

If you put on a façade to get someone to love you, and they do, you still don't feel loved—because you aren't being the real you. You may reason that they must not be telling you the truth. And if they aren't telling you the truth, they must not be trustworthy. Now you have trust issues, and you think it is the other person's fault. The arrows of apathy, anger, and blame have been shot.

When you abandon yourself and your interests, hobbies, and desires to please someone else, you disconnect from your True Self. Self-esteem issues arise because you are unhappy with yourself (while blaming the other person). When your self-esteem and self-respect falter, you don't feel worthy of the love you are seeking. When you don't feel like you deserve the love someone is trying to give you, you may subconsciously sabotage the relationship to prove yourself right by prompting the other person to leave you: *I knew it, he/she didn't really love me. I'm not good enough.*

On the flip side, when someone is seeking our love or approval we typically find it draining and annoying. It feels like they are trying to get something from us rather than share something with us. We start to judge them and tell them they need to change, and the ego drama of approval and control begins.

The ego-needs for approval and control can look a lot alike, and ultimately it doesn't really matter which one you are participating in. What does matter is that you start to notice what you are doing. You are operating from ego.

If you are operating from the need for approval, the remedy is to love and approve of yourself. When you are operating from the need for control, the remedy is to love and accept yourself and everyone else. Ultimately, we all need to do both. That is what authentic love is all about.

 **THE INVITATION** *Notice*

In what situations do you feel a need for approval? Do you seek acknowledgement from others? Do you second-guess and question yourself? Do you do what other people think you should do instead of what you want to do because you fear disappointing them? Do you take care of others but not yourself? Do you do things for others and then resent them?

Again, just like before, this is not an invitation to judge what you do, only to observe what you do and when you do it. Then, simply notice if acting from a need for approval makes your rela-

tionships stronger or weaker. Notice whether it makes you stronger or weaker. Notice whether the choice to defer your happiness and value makes you feel better and closer to others or worse and farther away. Notice if this choice of behaviors is working for you. Just notice.

11 How Relationships Work... and Then Don't

A dame that knows the ropes isn't likely to get tied up.
— MAE WEST

It is helpful to realize that the need for approval and the need for control are like opposite sides of the same coin, or two ends of the same magnet. Both become the clay that conceals our True Nature. Both cause the same outcome in relationships: Sooner or later they trigger Eros's arrow of apathy and indifference. The ego destroys relationships in its attempt to create them.

Sometimes it is hard to tell where one ego-need ends and the other begins, because they are intimately entwined. And we all succumb to both the need for approval and the need for control, flipping back and forth between the two sometimes even in the middle of the same situation. For instance, if you tell your partner that you want them to *tell you* they love you, you are seeking their approval while simultaneously trying to control when and how they communicate their love. Both sides of the ego can operate simultaneously.

Ultimately, it doesn't really matter which side you are leading with except for the fact that you will see the opposite effect in those around you and will likely want to blame them. The problem is that you end up feeling like a victim when in fact you have the power to change the situation. All you have to do is stop magnetizing the behaviors you are drawing from others by shifting how you show up in your interactions with them. (Part Four, "The EROS Equation," goes into detail about how to do this.)

Let's look at this dynamic more closely. Typically, one partner or the other (let's just say the woman, but it definitely can be the other way around and is not limited to heterosexual relationships) exhibits a need for approval. She is seeking her life mate—someone who wants her enough to marry her. She sees a man across the room who presents a need for control. They are drawn to each other—like opposite ends of two magnets. She does everything she can to make him like her, which may include, over time, giving up her friends, her family, her passions and interests. Perhaps he didn't even ask for or expect all this sacrifice. Still, she changed herself in an effort to ensure that he loved her. Initially, he happily receives all she is offering. They cruise along contentedly in an ultimately dysfunctional ego dance masquerading as love. It works...for a while.

Unfortunately, while she is giving and changing and trying to get approval from him—an external source—she is simultaneously disconnecting from her true, internal source of approval. The farther she moves away from her authentic self, the less love she feels from him and the more needy and demanding of love and attention she becomes. Since the magnet of her need for approval is so strongly activated, it evokes his need for control even more intensely. Thus, he may become even more demanding and critical.

The problem with the need for control, as I said before, is that control is impossible to achieve. We have all heard some variation on the wise saying "You can't change someone else." Try as we might to change another, they only change if they want to change, and even then they may not change. Even if it appears they are changing for you, if it is done from a need for approval, it is not authentic, and resentment or retaliation will eventually result.

When the retaliation starts, she may think she is coming into her own power and standing up for herself. In actuality, if she has not evolved in her awareness, all she is doing is flipping the ego magnet around and now operating from her need for control. She starts telling him how he needs to change; she nags, criticizes, and demands change. Or she gets revenge behind his back by doing whatever she wants to do. Or both. He then turns his magnet around and tries to accommodate her to keep her, or he activates his ego-need for control even more strongly, and they repeatedly get into fights.

Our couple is now engaged in a constant ego dance, with her presenting the need for approval and him the need for control, followed in an instant (or a day or month) with a magnetic shift. Now his need for approval and her need for control are triggered. Then they both flip into the need for control. Then they break up.

With great dismay that they ever allowed themselves to get into this situation, they silently vow never to date or marry (or hire or work with) someone like *that* again. They each re-enter the dating world with their need for approval or need for control fully activated and restart the whole process.

THE
INVITATION

Learn from the Past

Take a look at yourself and your previous (or current) relationships. Notice if you can see a pattern of battles for approval and control. Which ego magnet were you operating from? Did it switch? When? Can you see the approval and control drama taking place? Can you see it in your relationship with your parents? Your kids? Your coworkers?

The first step to turning this pattern around is to simply become aware of it. While it may not feel very good to look at these dynamics, once you recognize the ego at work in your love life you will begin to see that others are controlling you or seeking your approval because of the magnet you *are presenting. Seeing this will allow you to begin experimenting with transcending your ego—demagnetizing it—and aligning with your authentic self, your True Nature. You will immediately notice people responding to you differently. Experiment to see if what I am saying rings true.*

12 Restoring Balance and Authenticity

> *How to get rid of ego as dictator and turn it into messenger and servant and scout, to be in your service, is the trick.*
>
> — JOSEPH CAMPBELL

One of the goals of this book is to guide you through the process of reclaiming your True Nature so that you are no longer swayed by ego magnets—either yours or others'. I want to help you find your center, your place of balance, where you can be authentically responsive to the moment, rather than swinging between ego-needs.

The goal is to be internally motivated, to seek wisdom and guidance from within. When we seek solutions outside of ourselves, we blame things outside of ourselves for our problems. When we seek validation or identity outside of ourselves, we lose our sense of self. When we lose our sense of self, healthy relationships are impossible because we are the primary ingredient—the common denominator—in our relationships. When we are able to access our heart and soul, we access the wisdom, strength, compassion, discernment, intuition, and guidance to navigate relationships in a healthier way.

Consider how your bathroom scale periodically needs to be recalibrated to zero in order to operate accurately. If you neglect to do this, slowly but surely the scale will get farther and farther out of balance until it is totally inaccurate. If you never do it in the first place, the scale may always be off. The same is true for us humans. If we spend a few moments every day reconnecting with our authentic "golden essence," we recalibrate to a state of peace, strength, creativity, and wisdom. Every day that we miss this practice, we get a little farther from center, a little farther out of balance, until we forget entirely that we have a happy, peaceful source within. Suddenly, we find ourselves unable to cope, and our lives are in turmoil and chaos.

By way of a visualized example, I imagine my authentic self to be shaped like a heart. When I am not being triggered by my ego, I settle into my center, my heart. I feel balanced and peaceful. If, however, I get caught up in my ego-needs for approval, my heart shape shifts out of balance to the left. If I get caught up in my ego-needs for control, my heart shape shifts out of balance to the right.

When a couple or an individual comes for coaching, it's as though I can literally see their ego operating. And then when a shift takes place, I can see their authentic self. I call it "the hards" or "the softs," and it actually shows up on their faces. When we are in our egos, we feel hard, inflexible, unmovable, stuck, and/ or uncomfortable. In fact, being stuck in ego is a fairly unpleasant experience. It may feel like resistance, anger, hurt, or fear. When we are in our spirits we feel softer, more flexible, more understanding, compassionate. We experience a sense of freedom. It is far more comfortable, lighter, and more pleasant.

Resetting your zero, or coming back into balance, into your authenticity, requires practice for most of us. There may be a million ways to it, but the Six Essential Life and Love Skills, detailed in Part Six, have worked best for me. Practicing these skills will help you bring your "heart shape" back into balance. It will help you "reset your zero."

The reason balance is so important is because, as Einstein pointed out, it is difficult if not impossible to solve problems from the same state of mind that created them. Some sort of shift has to happen, whether it is a new perspective or the use of new skills, tools, or resources. When you access your True Nature you become resourceful—that is, "once again full of source." When you have access to your source, you become creative. Creativity is a huge benefit when trying to resolve problems as it allows you to see multiple solutions instead of myopically clinging to only one solution—which is usually a belief that someone or something outside of yourself has to change.

Let's see how a simple shift can change things. It turns out that what you say or do doesn't matter as much as what part of yourself you're coming from in terms of the ego magnet. For instance, if you're coming from your need for approval when you tell your partner that you love him or her, you are really trying to get them to say "I love you" in return. In seeking their validation, you may evoke their need for control, and you may find that they get irritated or even judgmental of you.

If you tell your partner, "I love you" from your need for control, you are really saying, "I love you, therefore you need to…." You're issuing an unspoken "to do" list necessary for your partner to deserve your love.

But if you say, "I love you" from a place of balance, it won't matter what your partner does or whether they say they love you in return. You are complete, either way. You will authentically know that you are loved.

When you are in balance, your ego magnet does not attract opposite ego reactions from others. You do not trigger people's criticism or their self-doubt. Don't just believe me. Play with these ideas. Experiment with them. Practice them. See what happens.

♥ THE
INVITATION *Find Your Balance Point*

Watch what happens when you do the exact same thing from a different part of yourself. For instance, imagine we were together and you started to cry. If I offered you a tissue from my need for approval, I would really be saying, "Aren't I kind and wonderful to offer this tissue to you? Could you please acknowledge my thoughtfulness?" This could evoke your need for control in such away that you find yourself judging me for offering you a tissue. You may not even understand why it bothers you so much because on the surface it looks like a kind gesture.

If I offer you a tissue from my need for control, I am really saying, "I'm uncomfortable with your emotions and tears. Clean it up and stop crying"—even though all I actually did was hand you a tissue. Through my evoking your need for approval, you may find yourself embarrassed and feeling shame, quickly wiping away your tears, blowing your nose, and trying to pull it together to meet my unspoken demands.

If, on the other hand, I drop into my authenticity before doing anything, I may find that the best move is to simply put the box of tissue where you can see it so you can be responsible for yourself. Or I may choose to hand you a tissue, but there will be no magnetic pull between us. Either you will take the tissue or not, but the interaction will not be loaded with my needs and agenda.

Since you don't want to be a victim of the way others approach you, being aware of the ego-need that is triggered by another can allow you to realize that you need to bring yourself back into balance. In essence, you don't have to choose to take the ego-bait dangling before you.

Can you notice how you feel when others provoke your ego? How does it differ from how you feel when you provoke theirs? Can you find the place within you that doesn't have an ego-driven agenda? Can you find the place that calls both of you to rise to your highest selves? This requires not only taking responsibility for yourself, but also allowing others to take responsibility for themselves—for instance, by holding the expectation that if the other person needs a tissue, they will get one or ask for one. When you take responsibility for yourself and allow others to be responsible for themselves, you demagnetize the ego magnet.

PART FOUR

THE EROS EQUATION

*Power is of two kinds. One is obtained by the fear of punishment
and the other by acts of love. Power based on love is a thousand times
more effective and permanent than the one derived from
fear of punishment.*
— MAHATMA GANDHI

The EROS Equation is the formula for personal power and
healthy relationships. If you apply this equation to every aspect
of your life, you will eventually recognize your responsibility for
every aspect of your life. When you take responsibility, the options are limitless, the solutions attainable, and the love immea-
surable.

At first this idea may seem laborious, but with practice the
equation can be utilized in all situations, revealing creative solutions to every challenge.

13 Event + Response = Outcome & Solution

People typically think that events, circumstances, and other people are responsible for their experiences. We blame our kids when we blow up. We blame our husband or wife or sweetheart for our unhappiness. We blame our job for our lack of income or our busy-ness. We blame our parents for the way we turned out. As I've pointed out, we generally look outside of ourselves for the problem and thus expect something outside of ourselves to generate the solution.

We think we would be happy if only.... If only I were married. If only my spouse listened to me. If only I had a bigger house. If only the kids would behave. If only my partner were more open and communicative. If only I were single. If only I had another child. If only the children would move out. If only I had more money. There are a million things we think would make us more joyful—if only the world and other people would cooperate with our desires.

Remember, these are ego-generated beliefs designed to protect us by placing responsibility externally, on others and events. The truth is, however, that as long as you think someone else is responsible for what you are experiencing in your relationships and in your life, you feel powerless. This is where the EROS Equation comes in.

What E + R = O & S means is that Events (people and circumstances) alone do not create the Outcomes you experience. Events plus your Responses to them are what create the Outcomes and lead to the Solutions you want.

In the original version, E + R = O, the "E" stood simply for "Event," meaning anything that happened. I have expanded the meaning of "E" from just Events to also mean Everyone Else, and, essentially, Everything External. The "E" is everything that happens outside of you. In the realm of relationships, this includes the behavior of others, everything they say or do. It also includes things that happen that aren't specifically generated by a person—for example, someone gets laid off, gets sick, gets accepted into a school, or gets a new job, or the economy changes.

An Event is simply what is; we have very little—if any—control over the events of our lives. We are generally powerless to change events because the minute they happen, they are in the past, no longer changeable, and they are often a result of other people's behavior—over which we also have no control. As long as we are trying to change the event, we are powerless.

The "R" stands for Response, Response-ability, or Reaction. I have narrowed down our response options to four types, including those that make you powerful and those that don't. This is explained in detail in Part Five, "The Response Options."

"O" is the Outcome or consequence (good or bad) that results from the combination of the Event and your Response to it. Outcomes can also be simply the way you end up feeling about the situation, or the resulting quality of your relationship, or whether you enjoy your job or hate it. The outcome is not necessarily, and in fact is often not, something you want. Some responses lead to outcomes you don't like, rather than to the solution you would prefer.

The "S" is the Solution that you actually want; it is the target, the goal. Knowing what you want makes it much easier to identify the Responses most likely to get you there. We will discuss identifying your desired targets in greater detail in Part Six, "Essential Life and Love Skills."

Let's review:

E — Event, Everyone Else, Everything External (what happens)

+ R — Response, Reaction, Response-ability (what you do, say, or think; the meaning you make)

= O — Outcome (how you feel and the resulting quality of the situation)

& S — Solution (what you want; a resolution to the problem)

In all my years as a relationship advisor, virtually every person who has ever come to me for coaching or has written a "Dear Eve" letter has said some variation on the following: "So and so is doing this [the E], and it makes me feel mad, sad, hurt, jealous, etc. [the O]." Then they ask, "How can I get so and so to behave differently [again the E] so that I can feel happy, satisfied, loved, etc. [the S]?"

Essentially, they are thinking Event = Outcome and have completely left out their Response. Thus, they never make it to the Solution. They have completely placed their power outside of themselves. They have abdicated responsibility for their happiness, blaming someone else for their emotional state and expecting someone else to fix it. As we've discussed, blame creates only victims and perpetrators and does not lead to change.

I always reply, "So and so is doing this [the E] and you are responding to it in a way [the R] that causes you to feel unhappy [the O]. What can you do differently [a different R] to create a different outcome and lead toward what you want [the S]?"

Reframing the situation empowers the person with the problem. When they access their authentic power, wisdom, intuition, discernment, and creativity and explore other responses, they will find the one that leads to the solution they seek. The Essential Life and Love Skills (Part Six) will help you with this.

Right about now, our egos rebel against this concept because it starts to see that the work that needs to be done is not up to the other person, but up to ourselves. In an effort to protect you, your ego may come up with statements of resistance like, *But it is their fault. He/she is the one who.... If only he/she would....* The ego has blinders on, and the only solution it can see is that someone or something else has to change.

But here is the bottom line: If you keep doing the exact same thing (the R), you are going to keep getting the exact same result (the O). Doing the same thing over and over while expecting different results is a definition of insanity. And, unfortunately for most of us, we allow the ego, with its need for approval and control, to call the shots on how we respond to others in a manipulative attempt to love and be loved. I am hoping that by now you clearly see that this approach simply does not work.

When we are stuck in our heads, we get cut off from our hearts. But when we can access our hearts, we are able to use our heads.

When you access your authentic power, you step into a creative state that allows you to see numerous, if not infinite, possibilities. We will look at various possibilities and their likely outcomes in Part Five, "The Response Options."

Do the Math

Take any situation, any event, and work through this equation. What happened (what was the Event)? How did you respond? What was the result (Outcome)? What did you want (Solution)? Every time you start to think that someone else should have done something differently, come back to your power and explore the options. See if you can find new ways to respond that create powerful results.

14 *Putting EROS to Work*

> *Love is as love does. Love is an act of will —*
> *namely, both an intention and an action.*
> *Will also implies choice. We do not have to love.*
> *We choose to love.*
>
> — M. SCOTT PECK

The EROS Equation can be applied to absolutely anything. If someone says something mean or calls you a name, that
is the Event. The event does not equal how you feel. It is ultimately not what the other person said that makes you feel bad; it
is what you think and do in response to it. You have choices. You
can agree with them and be hurt that they pointed it out. This
will make you feel sad. You can disagree with them and be mad
that they were so rude. This will make you angry. You can dismiss them as unpleasant or unkind. This may leave you feeling
neutral or judgmental. Or you can think, *It doesn't matter what they
think of me, I know my value*. This may uplift you. The Events do not
hold the power. Your Responses do.

Let me give you another example of how EROS works. Several
years ago, on my birthday, my husband took me out to dinner.

We got all dressed up, and since we live in Hawaii I was wearing several beautiful flower leis that friends had given to me. On the way to dinner, my husband wanted to stop at the hardware store to pick up something. As we left the store, we walked past a hotdog stand just as the worker was closing up shop. She reached down to unplug the water hose that connected her cart to the spigot. Apparently she had forgotten to turn the water off because a surge of water came pouring out of the faucet, drenching my husband and me. Being ever so much quicker than I, my husband darted away while I, not realizing what was happening, hesitated for a moment. Since it all happened so quickly, once the girl turned off the water we went into a sort of altered state that caused us to slow down and make a conscious decision about how we wanted to respond instead of just reacting reflexively. Getting sprayed by water was the Event, and we were trying to determine (without realizing it) what our Response would be, which would make or break the quality of our experience—the Outcome and Solution.

One of us suggested that we should be indignant and demand something from the hotdog stand, but the other pointed out that a lifetime supply of hotdogs wasn't going to serve us very well since I didn't eat red meat and he ate few hotdogs. Then we considered yelling at the girl for being so stupid, but she was really young, and if we'd had a teenage daughter who'd made such a mistake we wouldn't want people treating her poorly. That option wasn't in alignment with our True Natures. We discussed how we should be really angry, but it was my birthday and I didn't want to be angry. That option wasn't in alignment with the target of having a pleasant evening. Coming up with no other suitable ideas that would create an outcome we wanted, we decided to respond by accepting that we were wet, laughing about it, and going home to change clothes before setting out to dinner again. That is exactly what we did, and we ended up having a wonderful evening—and a funny story to tell.

The Event was getting sprayed by water. The Response was to laugh and change clothes. The Outcome and Solution were an enjoyable evening.

You can imagine how that evening could have gone in a very different direction if we had chosen a different response. We could have chosen to be angry, and the result would have been to get in a really bad mood. We could have insulted the girl and made her feel horrible. I could have responded by blaming my husband, because it was "his fault" we were at the hardware store in the first place (never mind the fact that I'd agreed to go). He could have criticized me for not moving out of the way of the water. Bottom line: We could have escalated the whole event into a series of horrible outcomes by employing blame as a response. The point here is that the Event would have been the same either way—it would not have changed. The only thing that changed the Outcome we experienced was how we chose to Respond to the Event. Although in this case my husband and I took time to consider our choices due to our shock, the truth is that we humans have the option to choose how to respond to every situation that life (or our partners, friends, relatives, etc.) presents to us.

This recognition of choice is the very quality that allows someone who has endured a truly challenging circumstance— such as rape, fire, serious illness, child abuse, a physical handicap—to overcome it and go on to have a fulfilling life or make huge contributions to society with the wisdom they've gained. A person who does not understand the power of choice ends up feeling like a victim of his or her life circumstances. A sense of powerlessness takes over and depression or aggression sets in. The result (outcome) is not caused by the event; it is caused by the person's response to the event. Please don't think I am downplaying the seriousness of certain life situations, or the challenges involved in recovering from tragedy. I'm saying that we always have a choice about whether or not to be defeated by what happens.

We are responsible for the outcomes we create and the solutions to our circumstances.

In relationships, this equation, Event + Response = Outcome & Solution, is especially powerful. Let's phrase it another way that has to do with relationships in particular:

The Other Person + Your Response to the Other Person = Your Experience & Your Goal for the Situation

A few years into my marriage I began resisting being married. Suddenly everything my husband did made me mad. In terms of the ego magnet, I had unknowingly come to the relationship with a need for approval, while he had more of a need for control. In this way we were perfectly matched, and it worked well for a while. But one day I switched my ego-magnet polarity and started trying to change and control him. The resulting battle of the egos simply did not work. Our relationship began to seriously decline, and I began to think about leaving. At the same time I felt completely trapped—by being married, owning a house, the dog, the cat, our business. The more trapped I felt, the more my ego was triggered to try to protect me and the worse things got.

One night I woke up literally and figuratively. Lying in bed I realized that I had been blaming the event (my husband) and not taking responsibility for creating a healthy, harmonious relationship. I realized that I had not been authentic, had let my ego run amok, and had totally lost sight of the target. Although I taught others the EROS Equation, I hadn't made use of my own remedy in this situation. I could clearly see that I had taken the path of resistance and that it was not leading toward any sort of solution.

Right then, in the wee hours of the morning, I decided to put the EROS Equation to the test. I decided to take 100 percent responsibility for my reactions to my marriage and my husband.

I wanted to see if I could fall back in love. I didn't believe it was possible, but I decided to allow myself six months to give the equation and my marriage a fighting chance. I had nothing to lose by trying, and everything to gain. I didn't tell my husband what I was doing because I didn't want to consciously or unconsciously expect him (the Event) to change. I wanted to see if I was powerful enough to bring about the change myself. I knew that if the EROS Equation worked, he would naturally change in response to me, but not because I was trying to change him.

I carefully monitored my responses to him. I chose words, thoughts, and actions that were in alignment with the goal of a loving, harmonious relationship. I could not believe how quickly things changed. When I treated him differently (without my ego magnets trying to manipulate him), he had the opportunity to respond to me differently. In a matter of days we set down our emotional "weapons," capable of inflicting pain, and began to rebuild a kind, loving, and joyful relationship. I quickly fell back in love with my husband. Now, after more than twenty years, I love him more every day. I continue to use the EROS Equation and the Essential Life and Love Skills daily as my personal practice.

This is my invitation to you: Choose your responses wisely in alignment with what you want to create. We have no control over another person or their behavior. Our power lies entirely in our ability to choose our responses to the person or event.

THE INVITATION | Explore Your Previous Responses

In order to take a new approach you have to know what your old approach was. Think about any situation that has happened in your life. How did you respond to it? Begin to consider what other responses you could have chosen that would have created different results. What other meanings were possible?

Practice self-observation, and identify your responses to current events. Notice what you are and aren't doing so you can make adjustments. Notice when your ego-needs lead your responses. Notice the meaning you have made about an event and whether it is even true. Remember, this exercise isn't about finding fault; it is about finding power—not power over other people but power over yourself, your choices, your experiences, and your future.

PART FIVE

THE RESPONSE OPTIONS

Alice came to a fork in the road.
"Which road do I take?" she asked.
"Where do you want to go?" responded the Cheshire Cat.
"I don't know," Alice answered.
"Then," said the Cat, "it doesn't matter."
— LEWIS CARROLL, ALICE IN WONDERLAND

The key to the EROS Equation lies entirely in your choices. Above all else, the equation shows that the Event is not where your power resides. Your power is in your ability to choose Responses that are in alignment with where you want to go.

We basically have four choices when we encounter an Event we don't like. This section outlines those choices and shows which ones work in the realm of relationships and which ones don't.

15 Negotiation

> *Negotiation in the classic diplomatic sense*
> *assumes parties more anxious to agree*
> *than to disagree.*
>
> — DEAN ACHESON

In applying the EROS Equation to your life, the first step is to identify which part of the problem is the Event and which part is your Response. This should be relatively easy because an Event is something external—what another person is doing or saying, or something that has happened. The Response is your part in the situation.

We have essentially four response options when an event occurs or when we encounter a behavior we don't like in another person:

1. We can **negotiate** to change the other person's behavior or the event.

2. We can **resist** the other person or the event and stay in the relationship.

3. We can **accept** the other person's behavior or the event and stay in the relationship.

4. We can **get out** of the relationship (or change the nature of the relationship).

I will explain each of these options in the coming chapters. As you read, see if you can recognize the responses you tend to default to.

Negotiation, the first option listed above, is an effort to change a situation, future events, or the other person (the Event). Negotiation is usually where we start when we don't like what someone else is doing (or not doing). Although we have no control over what another person chooses to do, and even though people do not change easily, sometimes people will change their behavior upon request. Depending on what you want changed, negotiation may work if you are explicit about what you are trying to accomplish.

However, note that with this option you are still putting the power for your happiness in someone else's hands. If they change due to the negotiation, you will be happy. If they don't, you won't. It is reasonable to attempt negotiation; just know that in so doing you are expecting the "E" to change, and it may or may not work.

How you approach negotiation has a great impact on its success. Remember, the idea here is to solve the problem, not complain about it. If you ask for change from your ego-need for approval or control (both of which are variations on the assumption "If you love me, you will..."), you will likely evoke a charged ego response that you don't really want. And, in some cases, it is possible that the other person cannot honor your request for reasons that are physical, emotional, spiritual, or mental—or maybe even due to memory issues.

One woman shared that she and her husband had several cats who liked to drink out of the toilet and would leave wet paw prints all over the toilet seat. This drove her husband crazy, so he asked her to keep the toilet lid down. She agreed that this made great sense and was fully willing to abide by his request. And yet nine times out of ten she forgot to do it. If the husband's only solution was her changing her behavior or the cats' changing theirs, he was going to be a victim. If, instead, she did her best to remember and honor his request while he simultaneously made sure the seat was dry before sitting on it, there would be no problem. (This situation is a variation on the age-old "toilet seat down or up" issue facing men and women the world over.)

Let's look at how negotiation works—or doesn't work—for an issue that might affect you on a daily basis. As an example, let's say your partner doesn't do dishes. You can certainly negotiate by asking your partner to help with the dishes. However, he or she may not enjoy doing dishes or may not want to do them; therefore, it is very possible that your request will not be honored—but it is still worth a try.

You might offer the solution, "How about if you do the dishes on Monday, Wednesday, and Friday? Or when I cook, you clean, and vice versa?" The challenge here is that even if your partner decides this is a fair request and is willing to do it, your happiness still lies outside of yourself (on the Event). Consequently, if your partner does the dishes on Monday and Wednesday, you will be happy and think your plan is working. On Friday, however, if he or she is tired from a long week and doesn't want to do the dishes, you will likely feel once again like a victim, only this time you may be doubly angry—once because your partner didn't do the dishes and twice because they said they would.

You might even be angry for a third reason, depending on your personal mythology and the meaning you have made out of his or her behavior. If you think your partner's failure to do the dishes means that he or she doesn't love you, you will react to that belief more strongly than you did to the dirty dishes. Then, when your partner thinks you are negotiating for the dishes to be done or are angry that they weren't, when in fact you're really negotiating for love and approval, the two of you are going to experience a communication breakdown.

Before you attempt negotiation, it is wise to practice some self-observation and evaluate your motives and the meaning you have made out of the situation. Are you asking your partner to change because the issue is really important, or are you trying to get approval or establish control? Be honest with yourself. It may be that all that is necessary in order to restore happiness is for you to let go of the issue.

For example, one woman's husband put the dishes in the dishwasher, but not the way she thought it "should" be done. She stopped and asked herself whether it really mattered, and had to admit that it did not. She realized it was far more important that she appreciate his efforts than correct him with her perception of the right way of doing things—especially since there isn't really a "right way" and a "wrong way" to load a dishwasher; there is just "her way" and "his way."

Sometimes, the things we want others to address are deeply imbedded behaviors, a lack of consideration or thoughtfulness, or major differences in values that aren't easily changed. We may also want another to change things that he or she may not want to change or may not believe can be changed. At times, our expectation that another person needs to change can hurt their feelings or cause them to get defensive. The whole scenario can leave you feeling powerless because, again, you have no control over the other person (the Event).

You do, however, have control over the state of being you bring to the negotiation table. This is where knowing your True Self will really serve you. Knowing your values helps both in negotiating with a partner and also in knowing what you are and are not willing to change in yourself at a partner's request. We will explore your true nature more in Part Six and look more closely at values clarification in Part Seven, "The Guideposts of Integrity." For now, keep in mind that although it is reasonable to attempt negotiation, its success is determined not by you but solely by whether the other person wants to and is able to change.

Experiment

Notice how well negotiation has worked for you so far. How have others responded when you've requested changes in their behavior? How have you responded to their requests for changes in you? Can you identify times when you made meaning out of the need for change that didn't really match the situation?

When considering situations that you deem need changing, first notice what you think the situation means. Then look at whether the actual situation needs to change, or simply the meaning you make out of it. If change is needed, consider whether, if you made the exact same request for change from your authentic self instead of from the ego, you would be met with a different response. Experiment with the part of yourself that is doing the negotiating, and see if you can authentically influence the outcome.

16 Resistance

> *Pain is a relatively objective, physical phenomenon;*
> *suffering is our psychological resistance to what happens.*
> *Events may create physical pain, but they do not in*
> *themselves create suffering. Resistance creates suffering.*
> *Stress happens when your mind resists what is... The*
> *only problem in your life is your mind's resistance*
> *to life as it unfolds.*
> — DAN MILLMAN

When we opt not to try negotiation or when it doesn't work, what virtually all of us do next is to respond by resisting "what is." Resistance takes place when we don't like something (the Event) and yet choose to stay in the relationship anyway. By "resist," I mean we get upset and/or complain about the behavior or situation; we may even try to deny that it is the way it is. In any case, we are convinced that the "E" or the other person has to change. Since we can't figure out how to get him or her to change through conscious methods, the ego gets triggered to protect us, and it tries to "help." So we resort to a series of relatively unconscious strategies to manipulate the other person into changing. The activated ego magnets of approval and control only make things worse.

Resistance is really an unskilled attempt to negotiate for change. This Response (which we generally engage in unconsciously) inevitably results in one or more of the following behaviors: nagging, barbed comments, sarcasm, ridicule, put-downs, arguing, withdrawal, passive-aggressiveness, unpleasant gestures, sulking or pouting, fighting, resentment, or revenge—all of which lead to unhappiness as the Outcome, and none which are in alignment with the Solution we want. When we enter a state of resistance, we get locked into control battles in which there are no winners. The choice to resist the other person always leads to the Outcome of blocking the flow of love and killing the joy in relationships. The result is always pain.

Back to the example of doing the dishes: If you go into resistance because your partner doesn't do dishes, your ego will try to change that reality. You may resort to making sarcastic comments, maybe putting your partner down in front of other people, or criticizing him or her. When you do the dishes, you may display passive-aggressive behaviors like clanking them loudly to make sure your partner knows you're unhappy. The more you resist, the more angry and resentful you become and the more angry and resentful your partner becomes. You might even withhold intimacy or communication because of your anger.

The two of you are no closer to having the dishes done, and now you're also mad at each other. The expression of love between you is damaged—not because your partner didn't do dishes, but because you chose to respond with resistance.

When we resist another person's behavior by making sarcastic comments, delivering put-downs, nagging, or whatever, we are hoping the other person will "get a clue," change their behavior, and do what we want them to do. The insanity is that our ego-minds think that if we are just mean enough, rude enough, critical enough, or withdrawn enough the other person will honor our desire for change. But it doesn't work, or doesn't work for long. And because this response option focuses on changing the other person or the Event, we are once again rendered powerless.

Resistance is always what causes suffering. Virtually every single person or couple I work with comes to me in a state of resisting how things are or how someone in their life is behaving. Every single one. Plain and simple, resistance makes things worse. I have never, ever seen this Response resolve a problem. In fact, it typically aggravates it.

Resistance is the option that the ego automatically chooses. Responses to an event that are based in ego always block love.

Resistance to another breeds resistance in return. Resistance leads to resentment and resentment leads to revenge. I'm sure you can see how poisonous these arrows are to a relationship.

When we get stuck in resistance, our natural inclination is to "get out," which is option number four, because the ensuing discomfort and displeasure loom so large it seems there is no other option. However, there is always another option, or at least one that should come first: acceptance, the topic of the next chapter.

THE INVITATION | *Take Aim*

Take a look at your attitude and behavior and ask yourself whether they are leading you toward your desired goal or Solution or away from it. Is your attitude building obstacles or clearing them? Next, realize that attitude is a choice. Sometimes we think the aim is to "teach them a lesson" or "show them who's in charge," but a misidentified target is a dangerous thing. Dive a little deeper into your heart. What do you really want? If love and connection are a part of the answer, the behaviors associated with resistance are not going to lead you there. Instead, take a deep breath and use your head and your heart together to see what other options emerge.

17 *Acceptance*

When we have walked the path of resistance and experienced the resulting devastation to the relationship, as I mentioned, our natural inclination is to skip to response option number four and get out. However, if we leave a relationship based on resistance, no evolution has taken place. All we have done is charge our ego magnets and then part ways, vowing to "never do that again" or "never date someone like her/him." When we re-enter the dating pool, however, with our ego magnets fully activated, we attract someone with the opposite charge and begin the process all over.

So before you take the leap of ending the relationship, explore the third option: accepting or acknowledging what is. Acceptance doesn't mean that the situation is necessarily your preference—simply that you accept that it is what is. You don't have to like that your family member is sick or dying to accept that they are sick or dying. You don't have to like that your partner does something, doesn't do something, or isn't capable of doing something to accept that it is so.

When you accept that changing certain things may not be in your power, you paradoxically become more powerful. When you let go of resistance and step into the creativity of your True Nature you begin to see what you can do to manage the situation.

As long as you resist the reality that your partner doesn't do dishes, you are still trying to find a way to get him or her to do them because it's the only solution you can see. Consequently, you are miserable (and, undoubtedly, so is your partner). But as soon as you truly accept the fact that your partner doesn't do dishes and you stop making him/her wrong—stop engaging in the battle to get him/her to change—you will start to see other options. For instance, you could just accept the fact that you are the one who washes the dishes and he/she handles other things you don't like to do—mowing the lawn, maintaining the car, fixing things around the house, cleaning, doing laundry, or paying the bills. This sort of division of labor has been employed throughout the centuries in households and businesses, and it is certainly a reasonable option. Or you could use paper plates, or hire a housekeeper, or eat out—or some combination of those options. On Monday you could hire someone, on Wednesday you could use paper plates, and on Friday you could go out. The point is that as soon as you stop resisting and accept what is, other options emerge that you couldn't see because of your resistance.

The ego sees only one solution: The other person has to change. The spirit sees creatively and identifies myriad Solutions.

For another perspective, consider what you would do if the other person *couldn't* change. What would you do if your partner literally couldn't do the dishes? I am certain if he/she had an allergy to dish soap, or two broken wrists, you would move into acceptance, stop being angry, and find another solution.

The reality is that whether you are accepting or resisting, your partner still doesn't do the dishes. The event doesn't change; only your experience of your relationship changes (as does his/hers).

Once you begin experimenting with acceptance, you may uncover some ironic twists to the situation. One woman shared that when she finally shifted into acceptance that her husband didn't do dishes, she began looking at her part in the dynamic. She realized that she had actually trained him not to do dishes! After all, he'd done dishes as a bachelor. But she had a need for approval, so once they moved in together, whenever he began to carry his dishes to the sink she would say, "It's okay, I'll do them," and let him watch TV instead. Without being aware she was doing so, she lovingly reprimanded him every time he tried to do the dishes. Voila! In just a short time she'd created a husband who didn't do dishes. Then, a few years later, her ego blamed him for not doing dishes.

If you want to create a harmonious, loving relationship, start by taking responsibility for your part in situations that bother you. Examine the meaning you are making out of the event and see if there is any reality to your interpretation. For instance, if the woman in our example concluded that her husband didn't do dishes because he didn't love her, she would be far too reactive to recognize the truth that her husband didn't do dishes because she had asked him not to. (In fact, he wasn't doing the dishes because he wanted to honor her original request.)

Another irony is that often when we stop trying to make someone change and we instead change our Response to them (when we drop the ego magnets), sometimes they just change on their own. The woman in our example noted that once she stopped caring that her husband didn't do the dishes, the more often she found him doing them.

When I was writing the book *Intellectual Foreplay: Questions for Lovers and Lovers-to-Be* (see Resources), I interviewed hundreds of people to see what they thought was important to ask a partner or potential partner. One woman told me I needed to ask "whether he likes the lights bright or dim in the bathroom." She explained that she and her husband got into a fight every morning and were on the verge of divorce over the light issue. She liked them bright so she could put on her makeup, and he liked them dim because he woke up slowly.

In truth, they were on the verge of divorce over resisting the other's preference, thinking the only solution was to change the Event. When we are able to accept what is, we see a multitude of other Solutions that cannot be seen through the blinders of ego—installing a dimmer switch, using the bathroom at two different times, moving into a home with two bathrooms, placing a makeup mirror in another room, or merely managing with the lights brighter or dimmer than you prefer without anger or resistance.

The same is true with the dishes. It is unlikely that you would leave your partner or get divorced over the dishes (or over the lights, or laundry, etc.). However, it is certainly possible that you could end up breaking up over the ensuing anger, fighting, manipulation, and hurt feelings that erupt if you continuously, day in and day out, resist the fact that he or she doesn't do dishes. The little things don't do us in; it is our Responses to the little things that make or break relationships.

When the other person is unwilling or unable to change, acceptance requires changing yourself instead of changing them. The change you make in yourself is to transcend your ego, realign with your True Nature, and make choices that contribute to the Solution rather than to the problem. When you let go of the need to control the other person's behavior, you are free to make a decision regarding what you want to do about it.

HOW DO YOU PREFER TO FEEL?

Acceptance feels like: forgiveness, apologizing, allowing, understanding, adjusting, compromising, serving, creativity, being discerning, moving away from, learning, growing, trusting, taking responsibility, asserting, gratitude. This is a case of the "softs" that I mentioned in Chapter 12.

Resistance feels like: arguing, fighting, sarcasm, blame, depression, put-downs, withdrawal, revenge, aggression, frustration, disrespectful gestures, passive-aggressiveness, intolerance, closed body language, distrust, resentment. This is a case of the "hards." These qualities describe the behaviors of ego.

Which qualities are more in alignment with your True Nature?

Acceptance is more easily understood over something simple like washing dishes. But what about the big issues like infidelity, gambling, abuse, drug addiction, alcoholism, money, and sexuality? The reality is that you still have to accept "what is" in order to figure out how to creatively respond to it. You still have to accept that your partner is an addict, or a gambler, or abusive, or doesn't want to be monogamous in order to figure out what you want to do with that information. As long as you resist the truth, you will get stuck in the quicksand of resentment and the quagmire of the need for approval and control.

The other person's behavior may not be right for you, and you may not think it is right for him or her, but you are not responsible for that part—that is the Event. As long as you keep focusing on changing the Event, you will create a negative Outcome. Switch your focus to your Response if you want the Outcome to be positive.

Once we step into acceptance, we may see that the only Solution is to get out. We will discuss this more in the next chapter.

THE INVITATION | Get Creative

When you find yourself in conflict with another, take a deep breath and let go of your need for control and your need for approval. Take another deep breath and accept what is; let go of resistance. Next, look for Solutions outside the influence of your ego. The only solution ego sees is that someone or something else has to change.

Can you allow the other person to be responsible for themselves? Can you speak in a softer way that is more aligned with your authenticity? Can you remove yourself from a dangerous situation? Can you let go of the problem? Can you simply accept the situation and release your anger and frustration? Can you find compassion for the other person? Can you take measures to protect yourself from the consequences of the other person's actions? Can you choose to honor yourself? Can you allow yourself to get out of the relationship without letting anger follow you?

Allow your creativity, flexibility, intuition, and wisdom to solve the problem. Then, rather than looking outside for the source of your problems, look inside for the source of your Solutions. Relationships require a lot of work, but rarely, if ever, is the work on the other person.

18 Getting Out

> *Some people believe holding on and hanging in there are signs of great strength. However, there are times when it takes much more strength to know when to let go and then do it.*
>
> — ANN LANDERS

The fourth option is to get out. There are times when leaving a relationship is the only truly viable option—especially when your or another's safety is at risk or when the issues absolutely go against your core values. Although leaving is always an option, it is not usually an easy one. There are certainly relationships that either have run their course or should not have been relationships in the first place. Such a scenario makes it easier to decide to leave. Keep in mind that there is a huge difference between getting out of a casual relationship or a job and getting out of a marriage or a long-term relationship. Some relationships are much more challenging to remove yourself from due to children, families, finances, or emotional entanglements.

If you decide that getting out is the response option you are going to choose, it is important that you still first "accept what is." If you decide to leave your spouse, partner, or job—or even your child, family, or parents—over something you are resisting, your resentment, your anger, and your hurt may get stuck in your system, causing your ego magnet to be more charged than ever. Once you re-enter the dating scene (or the job market, etc.), you then run the risk of repeating the pattern of resistance when a new partner (or coworker) does something that resembles the previous partner's behavior. The cycle starts all over again, with you trying to change Events outside of yourself.

On more than one occasion, in frustration over the inability to create a harmonious, loving relationship, people have confided to me that they were praying for their spouse to die or were considering suicide themselves as a means of getting out. In truth, what they wanted was a healthy relationship—or a divorce—but the actions (or inaction) they were considering totally missed either target. When we get our egos out of the way, we have so many options available to us. Leaving a relationship may not be easy, but sometimes it simply must be done, and indeed it can be done.

If you want to personally evolve and truly complete the relationship rather than drag it with you through time, you need to accept "what is" before or as you get out. Otherwise, your very resistance is likely to keep you in the relationship far longer than is healthy. Acceptance will set you free.

Believe it or not, when you shift into acceptance, you may even be able to come to peace with your partner's behavior as the perfect stimulus for you to learn something really important about yourself. You may feel gratitude that your partner's behavior set you free to explore a new phase in your life or to develop qualities in yourself that previously lay dormant. You may also see opportunities for getting out or discover other creative Solutions that you never saw before.

If you have already gotten out of an unhealthy relationship, it isn't too late to let go of any lingering resistance to the way things were and choose a new Response so that you can experience peace and acceptance and move forward freely.

THE INVITATION | Set Yourself Free

This is a great exercise to use when you are getting out of a relationship, letting go of a previous relationship, or even just regaining a sense of self in an existing relationship. After you read this, close your eyes and visualize yourself and the other person. Imagine that there is some sort of physical attachment connecting you to each other; visualize what form it takes. Where do you feel or see the attachment, and what does it look like? Some people see shimmering strings, some see claws or tentacles, some see ropes or chains. Some are attached heart to heart, mind to mind, or gut to gut, or perhaps the connection is genital—or all of the above.

These energetic ties are much like an umbilical cord between mother and child. After a certain point they drain both people. We sever umbilical cords to make both parties self-sufficient. In the same spirit of a desire for independence, visualize cutting the tie or removing the claws—whatever applies. You are welcome to use a symbolic tool, such as an imaginary light saber or knife, or to imagine removing the connection with your hands, or simply to visualize it retracting. Next, picture the healing of any severed parts belonging to you and the other party, and picture their re-absorption into their rightful owner. Now breathe.

You may only have to do this exercise once, or you may have to do it a thousand times. Whether or not you choose to stay in the relationship, there is a great power in symbolically allowing each person to be energetically responsible for him- or herself. This exercise is an important reminder to be self-sustaining and to wish the same for the other person. Whether you stay or leave, the freedom that comes from allowing this is often tangible.

PART SIX

ESSENTIAL LIFE
AND LOVE SKILLS

The Breeze of Grace is always blowing,
but you must set your sails to catch it.
— VIVEKANANDA

Learning to accept what is, step into authenticity, and see creative options requires a level of self-mastery. Self-mastery requires practice. The Essential Life and Love Skills described in this section comprise my personal practice—one that I superimpose over everything. Using these skills doesn't require an hour a day or indeed any extra time set aside. It does require an intention toward constant mindfulness.

The Essential Life and Love Skills will assist you in mastering the EROS Equation. As you explore and experiment with them, you will find that all six can happen simultaneously, in the space of one breath, bringing you back into alignment with your True Nature. Then your decisions, actions, words, and thoughts are far more likely to lead you where you want to go.

19 *Remember (or Discover) Who You Really Are*

> *The privilege of a lifetime is to become who you truly are.*
> — C. G. JUNG

Through the course of nearly thirty years of personal and spiritual growth and study, I have identified six Essential Life and Love Skills that are critical for creating a joyful life and healthy relationships—with your loved ones, coworkers, yourself, and spirit. These skills work beautifully with the EROS Equation and in fact can be the steps you take to help you master your Responses. The skills are:

1. Remember who you really are.

2. Determine what you want.

3. Self-observe.

4. Choose to let go.

5. Recalibrate to your authentic self.

6. Take actions in alignment with who you are and what you want.

Over the next few chapters I will explain each of these skills more fully, beginning in this chapter with the first one: Remember who you really are.

Trying to "remember who you really are" if you were never consciously aware of it in the first place is a little tricky. Thus, for some, "remembering" who you really are may actually seem more like "discovering" who you are.

As a labyrinth facilitator as well as a relationship specialist and coach, I believe the labyrinth is an excellent tool for self-discovery. While most people think of a maze when they hear the word "labyrinth," the two are not always the same. Take a look at the labyrinth pictured on the next page. It is a drawing of one that is inlaid in the floor of the Chartres Cathedral in France. It is not a maze. It has only one path leading into the center and back out. There are no choices about where to turn and no dead ends. Rather than a game to see if you can avoid getting lost, it is intended as a path of reflection along which you travel to seek and find your True Self.

Rather than going on and on about the power of walking the labyrinth, I'll refer interested readers to my book *Way of the Winding Path: A Map for the Labyrinth of Life*. For the purposes of this book, I share the labyrinth pattern as a symbol that can bring greater

Drawing of labyrinth inlaid in the floor of Chartres Cathedral, France

clarity to the concepts I am explaining. It is my experience that the sacred center of the labyrinth represents our authentic essence or True Nature (introduced in Chapter 4). We each have a sacred center that is still and ever-present, just like the one in the labyrinth. Yet we each also have the twisting, chaotic turns that surround the center and sometimes make us think we are lost. I equate the outer twists and turns of the labyrinth to the chaos of the ego-mind.

Our sacred center, or True Nature, if you will, is surrounded by the dramas we get caught up in regarding love, money, health, housing, career, family, etc. Just as we think we have life figured out, we encounter a 180-degree turn: We fall in love, have kids, suffer illness, grieve a loved one's death, land a new job, move to a new city. Both the "good" experiences and the "bad" ones can throw us for a loop. As we navigate life, we get lulled into believing that we *are* our various dramas. Sometimes we even forget that the sacred center, the sacred source, is available to us.

We begin to identify with our ego—our personality, our body, our looks, our roles, our job. In truth, we are more accurately (or at least are capable of being) spirit beings—loving, lovable, creative, wise, compassionate, forgiving, adventurous, capable—who have egos, personalities, bodies, roles, and jobs.

Merely setting the intention of discovering this aspect of ourselves triggers step one into action. The more you pay attention and look for the evidence of your True Nature, the more likely you will be to start noticing its signs. The signs may show up in serendipitous moments during which you are surprised by your intuition's accuracy, or the manifestation of something you were just thinking about, or a prophetic dream, or the clear answer to a prayer. It may show up in your talents or creativity or problem-solving abilities or through a great idea. A sense of who you really are may emerge when sitting quietly in nature or in a moment of clarity or laughter. Our authentic self is always with us, intending to serve us, and when we have a moment of getting out of our own way, we are able to experience it. I call these moments of connection "Divine Indigestion": that gnawing feeling that magic is in the air, that there is something more to life and more to each of us than what meets the eye.

Scuba diving is another great metaphor for this phenomenon. No matter how rough the conditions of the sea, if a diver drops just a few feet below the surface, he or she is treated to calm and tranquil waters. From this vantage point, the diver can look up to the surface and watch the waves breaking above—without being a part of the chaos. Our true essence is the same. No matter how much drama we have going on in our lives, our spirit is always calm, connected, and capable. It is unaffected by our ego dramas.

When we become adept at recognizing the true essence of our beings, we also become adept at recognizing the behaviors that are generated from the ego.

It is said that when Michelangelo was asked how he managed to carve the statue of David out of a huge block of marble, he explained that he simply visualized David. Then he carved away everything that was not David.

Much akin to chipping away the clay on the giant golden Buddha, getting reacquainted with our authentic self allows us the opportunity to begin to "carve away" everything that has built up over time to protect us, but which doesn't truly serve us anymore. Rather than adding "clay" with unconscious behaviors, instead we begin the process of choosing our behaviors and responses. Even if they are the exact same behaviors as before, when we choose them consciously, we become powerful rather than victimized.

In the book *How to Know God,* the authors Swami Prabhavananda and Christopher Isherwood explain, "If the body is thought of as a busy and noisy city, then we can imagine that, in the middle of this city, there is a little shrine, and that, within this shrine, the Atman, our real nature, is present. No matter what is going on in the streets outside, we can always enter that shrine and worship. It is always open."

Taking the time to silently access your sense of authentic self is imperative to your self-mastery.

THE INVITATION | Feel the Difference

Simply begin to pay attention to the difference between who you really are and who you pretend to be. Take a moment to write down all the qualities you would use to describe your higher self as you imagine it would be, or as you already know it to be. Then take a close look at yourself to notice when you embody those qualities, if even just for a moment.

Notice the blessings and gifts that are bestowed upon you daily. Notice your talents and creative abilities. Also notice your feelings.

Find a moment or two every day to reflect, reconnect, give thanks for the magical moments, and enter the shrine within. Sit in silence and simply listen. Invite your True Nature to come forward, and create the space for it to do so. See if you can access the place within you that is peaceful, aware, and calm. You may be pleasantly surprised.

20 | *Identify Your Target*

> *The odds of hitting your target go up*
> *dramatically when you aim at it.*
> — MAL PANCOAST

    The second essential life skill is identifying what you want to create, what type of relationship you want to have, what qualities you want to embody, or what kind of life you want to live. In essence, what is the Solution you would like to aim toward?

    For the sake of this conversation, let's say the target is to create a loving, harmonious relationship—whether with yourself, your coworkers, or your loved ones. Even if a divorce or a breakup is inevitable, a harmonious and amicable one would be optimum, right? This seems like a no-brainer, but if you are in the middle of a fight, or on the verge of divorce, or sick and tired of the ego battle, it is not always easy to set your sights on the goal of creating a loving, harmonious, or respectful relationship.

    Having clarity about your goal is imperative. You can imagine that the problem-solving steps would be very different if the stated aim were to leave each other alone and never speak to each other again versus to heal the hurt and be friends or lovers again.

A client of mine shared that she was considering divorce, so we discussed her desired target. She thought into the future and realized she didn't know what she truly wanted. I asked her, "If I could wave a magic wand, do you want to be divorced right now?" She immediately answered, "Now? Today? Oh, no!" I asked, "Do you want to be miserable?" She laughed and said, "Of course not." So I responded, "Then right now, stay married and make the goal to be in a harmonious, loving relationship for now. When you come to the moment when you would answer the divorce question differently, then we will talk about divorce." Until then, she decided to make a healthy relationship the target.

Even when people know what their target is, when they self-observe (essential skill number three, discussed in the next chapter), they often are surprised to see that their words, thoughts, and actions are in exact opposition to their goal. Regardless of the target, it is important to align our behavior so that we are aiming toward it. This, too, can be trickier than it seems.

When you're dating, it helps to know if the goal you want is marriage, companionship, casual sex, or staying single. These very different targets will determine very different behaviors.

Once married, we need to identify the quality of marriage we want to create and also to notice the various mythologies or meanings we've formulated about marriage. We may be quite surprised to discover that our mythology differs from our spouse's.

Aside from relationships, it is my deep belief that we are all here in human form to discover how to be authentic—in alignment with our highest self—and how to direct our steps according to our personal values, goals, and ethics. If you aren't sure what you want in the realm of relationships, start by identifying what qualities you value and want in your life in general, and set your intention to live in alignment with them in spite of your relationship status. Part Seven, "The Guideposts of Integrity," will help you.

The power of identifying your target is that it allows you to know which way to go. The power of self-observation (the next essential skill) is that it allows you to see which way you are *actually* going.

THE INVITATION | Explore What It Is You Want

Determining what you want may require a little soul searching, but don't get caught in the trap of trying to figure out what you want for the rest of time, because that level of commitment usually triggers the ego into action. Start more simply. What do you want right now, in this moment? What qualities do you value in life, in yourself, in others? Can you identify an immediate target in the realm of your relationships? Can you commit to seeing what happens if you align your words, thoughts, and actions with that goal for the day? The week? The month? The next six months?

Pick a period of time that doesn't feel threatening to your ego, and try the goal on for size—even if it is only for this one instant. Can you align yourself with your target right now? How about now? And now? One moment always leads to the next. You can always change your goal if you have chosen the wrong one, but I have never seen "harmony and health" be the wrong choice in the realm of relationships—even if identifying that goal reveals a need to get out of the relationship.

21 Self-Observe

> *Self-observation brings man to the realization*
> *of the necessity of self-change. And in observing*
> *himself a man notices that self-observation itself*
> *brings about certain changes in his inner processes.*
> *He begins to understand that self-observation is*
> *an instrument of self-change, a means of awakening.*
> — GEORGE GURDJIEFF

Self-observation, the third essential skill, may well be the most important. It seems so obvious and so simple, and yet many of us are extremely unskilled and unpracticed at paying attention to our own thoughts and feelings. We tend to operate on automatic pilot, as if we have no control.

Practicing self-observation—noticing what we are thinking, feeling, saying, doing, and imagining—allows us to become self-aware. When we are aware of what we are doing, we realize we have choices, and choices are what make us powerful. In essence, when we know what we are doing, we realize that we have chosen to do it. When we take responsibility for our choices, we are no longer victims. If we don't like what we are doing, we discover options for doing something different.

The very act of noticing how we feel can allow us to release or let go of a stuck or stagnant emotion or a self-sabotaging habit. I once worked with a student who denied everything she was accused of by friends, teachers, or her parents. One day I said, "I want you to simply observe yourself and notice that you always deny what you do." Her immediate response was, "I do not." At which I laughed and said, "Notice what you just did!" I assured her this was not an assignment to change what she did or even judge herself, but rather to simply notice what she did. Her task was to become conscious so that she was aware of and choosing her behavior rather than operating unconsciously. From that day on, I never heard her deny her behavior again. Just the act of awareness released her from the habit—at least in front of me.

The more observant we are, the more we realize that there is a difference between the observed and the observer. Once, when I had just gone through a breakup with a boyfriend, I was lying on the couch sobbing. I heard a little voice in my head saying, "Wow, you are really crying. You haven't cried like this since you were a little girl." There was no judgment of my behavior, only an observation. Even in that moment of despair, I was aware that there was a part of me that was not sobbing or even feeling my pain. It was hard to keep crying and feeling sorry for myself once I knew that there was a part of me (my True Nature) that was not buying into my drama at all. Nor was it judging me. It simply observed, but the mere awareness of this part of myself held the invitation to choose to align with it rather than with the hurt and angry ego. The truth was that it was a wise decision to break up with this boyfriend, and there really was no reason to cry. Only my ego-needs for approval and control were not being met. My ego was in resistance. My spirit, however, was not upset at all. "It" just patiently watched and waited for my ego to catch up.

Our true, authentic selves are not caught up in our ego dramas. Our True Self stays calm and capable through everything we experience. When we know this aspect of ourselves, or watch for it, we can learn to tap into its strength when we most need it.

When we practice self-observation, we are able to see when we are behaving in alignment with our goals and values and when we are not. We notice when we are putting on a show for someone rather than aligning our behavior with the truth. We notice if we are smiling when we are actually sad, or if we say we are fine when we are not. We may notice if we are pretending to be mad when we really aren't, just to manipulate someone else's behavior. Or we may notice that we are thinking negative thoughts about ourselves, making us feel insecure. We notice when we are resisting what is and when we are accepting. We may even notice when we are truly content, peaceful, and joyful. Self-observation allows us to notice whether our behavior (Response) is leading toward our goals (Solutions) or away from them.

| THE INVITATION | *Familiarize Yourself with Your Self* |

Begin by simply asking: How am I feeling right now? What am I doing right now? What am I thinking right now? What am I saying right now? And notice the answers, however they arise. As you become adept at practicing self-observation, you will begin to notice that your thoughts create your feelings. If you feel bad, or hurt, or angry, or jealous, trace those feelings to what you are thinking and the meaning that you are making out of the events that have happened. You will likely discover that your thoughts, even more so than reality, are what are creating the way you feel. You will also discover that you can change your thoughts or the meaning you have made.

The most important aspect of self-observation is that it causes you to be aware. When you are aware you see that you have choices. When you have choices you are powerful.

22 | *Choose to Let Go*

> *Sometimes people let the same problem*
> *make them miserable for years when they*
> *could just say, So what? That's one of my*
> *favorite things to say: So what?*
>
> — ANDY WARHOL

     The fourth Essential Life and Love Skill is choosing to let go. This concept always brings up the question "What, exactly, are we letting go of?" The answer is "Anything that is not in alignment with your True Nature, your values, and your goals." It involves transcending the ego and letting go of resistance. As I've said, it isn't really that the ego is "bad"; rather, it is misguided. Unfortunately, most of us think we are our egos, rather than recognizing a deeper, more substantial aspect of our beings. Thus, if we haven't taken the time to explore who we really are, the idea of letting go or transcending the ego can be scary. Most of us don't know what would remain.

     Remember, as described in Part Three, "Ego Battleships vs. Real-ationships," all the behaviors of the ego are meant to protect you—the beautiful, pure authentic you. When you know who you really are, and what you want, and are self-observant, you will more easily see when you are operating from your ego-needs for approval or control. You will begin to see when what you are doing is leading away from your targets. That is when skill number four comes into play; it is the decision to change course, transcend the ego, and realign with who you are and what you want.

When someone does or says something that upsets us, our self-protective ego will always suggest we retaliate by putting the other person in their place, being critical back, arguing, and the like. If we simply ignore our ego, repressing the need for protection, it will get louder. If we honor the ego and do what it suggests, we will destroy or damage our relationships. Instead, acknowledge the ego's concerns, listen to what it wants to do, and consider which direction that will lead. Watch the trajectory of that arrow to see where it will likely land. Then give equal time to your True Nature. Consider the target you actually want to hit, and listen to the plan your spirit devises for reaching it. Now you have the opportunity to choose your actions.

I would be lying if I said I always choose the path of my True Nature. However, because of my practice of self-observation I do know when I am choosing otherwise and the probable consequences that will come with that choice. Every single time I have honored the plan of my ego, I have shot the arrow of hurt into the heart of the relationship and created pain for another and myself.

Whenever you find yourself in conflict (resistance) with someone else, while remembering who you really are, observe yourself and notice what you are feeling and thinking. Notice whether you are experiencing a need for control or a need for approval. Remember, if you find that you are judging or trying to change the other person, your ego is displaying a need for control. Take a step back and realize that this is your ego's misguided attempt at love and that your ego is exactly what is blocking your ability to love—and also what is blocking creative solutions to the problem. Take a deep breath and let go of your need for control. The only person you need to control is yourself.

If, on the other hand, you are always wondering whether you are doing things right (or wrong) and are concerned about what people think of you, your ego is exhibiting a need for approval. Remember, this is your desire to be loved, but your ego's neediness actually blocks your ability to be loved. Take a deep breath and choose to let go of your need for approval. The only approval you need is your own spirit's. When you are in alignment with your higher, authentic self, the world will love you—and you will love yourself.

This is the process for transcending "resistance to what is" and practicing "acceptance of what is" and then determining what to do about it.

THE INVITATION | Let Go of Your Shiny Pennies

It is said that one method of hunting raccoons is to drill a hole in a log and put a shiny penny in the hole. A raccoon comes along, sees the penny, and, being the curious type, tries to retrieve the penny. The problem for the coon is that when his paw is cupped around the penny, he can't get his paw out of the hole. When the hunters come along, all the raccoon has to do to free himself is let go of the penny. The raccoon, however, so engulfed in his desire for the penny, never sees that his demise is inevitable due to his lack of willingness to let go.

What are your shiny pennies? What are you holding on to, demanding, expecting, or doing, that, if simply dropped, would free you? Consider the possibility that some of your pennies are merely beliefs from your personal mythology and don't actually hold the meaning you have assigned to them.

Whenever you're pondering a problem in your relationship with a family member or partner, coworker or boss, first look within and see if the source of conflict is merely a token you're clinging to, or if change truly needs to take place. If it is just an alluring but falsely precious trinket, with a little reframing or an internal shift, or by making new meaning, you can eliminate the problem.

The wonderful thing about reframing the problem is that often, once you've let go, a multitude of creative solutions will become apparent. Sometimes the other person will even naturally change their behavior once you stop letting it bother you or trying to change them. When we are most stuck on something, we are least likely to see options. Often, a Solution is as simple as dropping the penny. Then we may be surprised how differently we see our situation on the other side of the coin.

23 *Recalibrate to Your True Nature*

> *The authentic self is soul made visible.*
> — SARAH BAN BREATHNACH

The fifth step or skill is recalibrating to your authentic self. This step is very similar to step number one, remembering who you really are. However, remember as we might at the beginning of our day, it may not be long before we discover ourselves (if we are self-observant) acting like who we really *aren't*—angry, jealous, controlling, depressed, or full of self-doubt. Once we've made that observation, we have the opportunity to transcend the ego drama of control and approval and return to our authentic selves. Whenever you feel off-balance or out of sorts, return to center, return to your heart. You have the ability to do this any time, anywhere. All you need to do is observe, let go, and return to love—then take any necessary action from there. We may have to do this a thousand times a day.

We have already discussed the importance of remembering or discovering who we really are—that divine aspect of ourselves with which we are aiming to align our thoughts, words, and actions. Now let's look at why and how to realign with it.

Most of us have heard the suggestion to "be here now" or "be present." In fact, it is almost a cliché. In all honesty, however, few of us really understand why or how we need to do so. After all, most of us have issues from the past that need resolving and goals for the future that need attending. So what is the big deal about the here and now? I have spent years exploring this question and have come to some very powerful discoveries that will assist you in realigning with your True Self.

It is my experience that getting present—anchoring ourselves in the current moment—is how to open the door to our hearts, to our authenticity. In fact, I'd venture to say it is impossible to access our true essence when we are not present. Trying to do so is like driving down the road while looking constantly into the rearview mirror or focusing entirely on the map—and altogether missing where we are.

I liken the process of getting present to stepping into the center of the labyrinth (see Chapter 19). When we step into the labyrinth's center (which symbolizes our own center), we can see the drama surrounding us without engaging in it. We can see things from a different perspective, more like a bird's-eye view than a myopic one. We can see the path and where it leads more easily than we can when we are on it.

When we bring our awareness into the present, from a place of strength, calm, and power, we can manage the dramas surrounding us. If there is something from the past that needs attending to, we can take care of it with all our faculties available to us. Likewise, if there is something we need to alter in the present moment to realign our direction with the targets or goals we've set for the future, we will be able to adjust now, in the current moment. When we choose our Responses for managing issues from this grounded, centered place, we stand a good chance of resolving problems rather than contributing to them.

In the realm of relationships, the past (heavily steeped in our personal mythology and in the meaning we have made) has a nasty way of creeping into our minds and altering how we handle things. When our current partner behaves even remotely the way a previous one did, we may react with the force of a hurricane when a light rain shower, metaphorically speaking, would have sufficed. And when we are focused on the future instead of the present, we often become fearful and reactive about what might or could happen. In such circumstances, our behavior tends to contribute to bringing into reality the very thing we fear. I'll discuss fear in more detail in Part Eight, "Managing Emotions and Change." For now, let's turn our attention to how to let go and realign with the present, where we can access our authentic heart.

When we are immersed in ego, the focal point of our awareness is in our heads. Our soul, as discussed in Chapter 12, "Restoring Balance and Authenticity," gets tweaked out of shape. Notice when this happens, then take a deep breath and bring your awareness into your body. Notice your senses. Notice your breath, your posture, any sights, smells, sounds, and feelings. Return your awareness to the now. As soon as you do, you will likely feel more calm, centered, and creative. You will feel more able to consider a number of possible solutions rather than the one your ego suggests, which usually involves exerting some sort of manipulative force on someone else. What I'm describing can be likened to taking an elevator down from your head to your heart, and it can happen in one breath. Okay, sometimes two or three breaths, but usually all it takes is one. When you do it, you will access your sacred center, and an entirely different world of options will become available to you.

With a little practice, you can transcend your ego, step into the present moment, and feel the door to your heart open, where you can access your authentic strengths.

If you are not familiar with your authentic self, I assure you that it has been trying to make itself known to you. Note that the qualities of high self-esteem or authenticity often *look* like the qualities of ego—assertive, passionate, confident—but they *feel* very different. Behavior based in true self-esteem is never done with an intention to hurt or belittle others—only ego does that.

Pay attention to how you feel when you are with other people, and you will be able to tell if one or both of you are coming from ego or self-esteem. Do you feel hard, or soft?

The more you practice self-observation, letting go of your ego dramas, and bringing yourself into the present, the more you will realize that your dramas are temporary and generally self-created. And that your authentic self is unwavering, steady, constant, creative, capable, compassionate, and peaceful. With a little practice, you will be able to feel the difference in yourself and in your relationships.

 ## Practice — Take a Deep Breath and Notice the Now

You can practice anchoring yourself in the present moment absolutely anywhere, anytime. Experiment with bringing your awareness into your body. Notice your senses—what do you smell, hear, see, feel, taste? Pay attention to what you notice around you.

Experiment with discovering what brings you into the present (not counting any substances that might serve as an artificial means of doing so). Experiment with seeing if you can gain power over the "hards" and the "softs." To move from your head to your heart, all it takes is a single breath and your awareness.

24 Take Aligned Action

*Follow your bliss and the universe
will open doors for you where there
were only walls.*
— JOSEPH CAMPBELL

A man once lamented to me how difficult it was to meet single women on Maui, so I asked how he was going about it. As it turned out, he was traveling from home to car to work and back without going out at all. I offered some suggestions about how to get out where the single women were, but every option was met with an excuse as to why he could not, would not do it. Simply put, no action, no results.

Action, however, must be in alignment with what you are trying to create; hence, the sixth skill: Take aligned action. This is where choosing our Responses to Events comes in. We want to be sure our Responses are in alignment with the Solution we desire.

People regularly tell me that they want to create healthy, loving relationships, but often their actions, words, and thoughts are directly contributing to the exact opposite result. You cannot create a healthy, loving relationship when you are constantly thinking judgmental thoughts about your partner—or about yourself—or when you are withholding important feelings, being dishonest, or seeking love and attention outside of your agreement with your partner. You cannot create healthy, loving relationships when you are trying to control your partner or when you stop being who you really are or doing what you love in an effort to get his or her approval. Just as you cannot get to San Francisco by driving toward New York, you will not meet your goal when your behaviors don't lead in that direction.

Nor will you meet your goal by doing nothing. You can pray for, wish for, and visualize what you want, but your prayers are unlikely to be answered unless you take active steps toward what you desire. Even if the perfect person were to miraculously show up on your doorstep, you'd still have to get to know them, ask them out, and, if a relationship did develop, use the Essential Life and Love Skills and the EROS Equation to assist in making the relationship work.

The beauty here is that when we have already taken the other five steps, our actions are much more likely to be aligned and inspired. In fact, when we let go of our ego dramas, resources we never thought of often become obvious. As I've said, when we align with our authentic self, we become imaginative and see new Responses that lead to desirable Solutions.

When I was teaching school, I had a student whom the principal had assigned to me for five of the six class periods. His behavior had caused him to be removed from all the other teachers' classes. It took me a while but I finally realized that how I treated him each and every period made all the difference in our potential for a successful class. He would misbehave and treat me horribly during the first period. When the bell rang he ran out of the classroom and then returned late for the next period. If I used period two to punish him for his behavior during period one, I found I would get the exact same behavior, or worse, than I did before. He would match my (low) expectations. Regardless of what I actually said to him, if my energy and thoughts were judgmental, as if I were saying, "Well, look who decided to show up. I hope you are going to be better this period than you were last. If you don't, I am going to keep you in at recess," that need for control on my part would *guarantee* that we'd have a horrible second period.

If, instead, I took several deep breaths between classes, realigned myself with the goal of having a healthy interaction with the student, and brought myself into the present moment, I would be able to greet him when he returned as if we'd never had an encounter that day. I had to actively work to allow each class period to be a new opportunity for a totally new interaction with him. When he came in I would welcome him like any other student, ask how he was doing, and pretend it was the first time

I had seen him all day, even though he had just been in my class five minutes earlier. This allowed him the freedom to behave differently, and we stood at least a fifty-fifty chance that our interaction would go more smoothly.

As the saying goes, you never step into the same river twice (because the water is constantly moving). Likewise, you never truly encounter the same person twice. In between meetings, they have new ideas, new experiences, and new awarenesses— and so do you. When we align our actions with who we are and what we want, we also need to align them with what is happening in the present moment.

THE INVITATION	Practice the Essential Life Skills in Every Area of Your Life

Give your words and actions the "purpose test." Notice what you are saying and doing, and ask yourself if they are leading you closer to your goals or farther away from them. Consciously choose words and behaviors that move you toward your target. Aim to base your words and actions in love. Say and do things that make you, and those around you, feel more loving.

When something bothers you, take a deep breath and remember who you really are. Self-observe and notice what you are thinking, feeling, and doing. Identify whether your ego-need for approval or control (or both) is at work. Take another deep breath (or two, or three) and consciously choose to let go of that need, transcending your ego. Recalibrate to your authentic self, and choose your next steps in alignment with both whom you really are and what you are trying to create. Although all these steps may seem like a lot of work in the beginning, the more you practice, the more readily—even instantaneously—the whole process occurs. In fact, it can happen during the course of one deep breath. You can move beyond a drama-filled life and dramatically improve your mental and emotional health and your relationships.

PART SEVEN

THE GUIDEPOSTS
OF INTEGRITY

Your beliefs become your thoughts,
Your thoughts become your words,
Your words become your actions,
Your actions become your habits,
Your habits become your values,
Your values become your destiny.
— MAHATMA GANDHI

As you've probably gathered by now, honoring the EROS Equation is about making conscious decisions in alignment with what you truly want and who you really are. When making tough choices, it is immensely helpful to know what you believe in, what your values are, and what rules you choose to live by.

When our values and ethics guide our steps, we may not always end up where we thought we would, but the journey will be immensely more satisfying. The following chapters will help you gain clarity about the guideposts that will point you toward your intended target.

25 *Define Your Values*

The guideposts we are talking about here assist you in choosing behaviors that will aim your Responses—words, thoughts, and actions —toward what you want to create. Identifying your values, writing them down, and defining what they mean can help you make decisions along the way. In essence, your values serve as guideposts for being authentic and having integrity in your actions.

In the realm of relationships, knowing your values—and recognizing and honoring your partner's values—is particularly helpful. One of the challenges we bump up against is the difference in what certain words mean to different people—even common words like "love," "marriage," and "family." You may be surprised by the contrast between two people's view of the same concept. Defining your values offers greater clarity.

Putting abstract concepts like "love" into words is not easy, but doing so is important to making sure that you and your partner are on the same page, using the same language, and getting your definitions from the same dictionary, so to speak. Sometimes it is easier to begin by determining what does *not* define a value. For instance, "Love is not possessive. Love is not jealous. Love is not confining or controlling. Love is not limited. Love is not judgmental. Love is not scary. Love is not dramatic. Love is not conditional." Then move on to what *does* define it: "Love is accepting. Love is appreciative. Love is supportive. Love is compassionate. Love is open and abundant. Love is the core essence of spirit."

There will be times when you discover that several paths could lead toward a certain Outcome; however, not all of the paths are in alignment with your beliefs, morals, and ethics. Therefore they don't truly lead to a Solution. For instance, if financial security is your goal, you could earn, invest, find, inherit, or borrow money. You could also deal drugs or steal. If your values include honesty and legality, then some of these options are automatically off limits. Still others may not be in your control, like inheritance. Likewise, if getting married is your goal, but you mislead someone, lie to them, or plan on trying to change them, you may end up marrying them, but neither of you will be happy. Bottom line: If you reach your target while employing means that lack integrity (e.g., if you cheat, steal, or lie), you may find that achieving the goal doesn't truly make you happy.

Prioritizing your values will help you make decisions when work and relationship, or relationship and spirituality, or marriage and children come into conflict. It is not necessarily important that you and your partner have exactly the same values, but it is important that you have complementary values. If one of you has career or wealth at the top of the list and family shortly thereafter, while the other has family at the top of the list and financial security shortly thereafter, this arrangement could be perfect for creating both financial security and a nurtured family. However, if one of you prioritizes family first and the other prioritizes family last, you could encounter constant conflicts—unless you look carefully at the difference and respond to the situation consciously.

One couple I worked with had two entirely different definitions of what "family" meant. This can be a challenge for a couple not only in creating their own family, but also in deciding how much time to spend with in-laws, adult children, and extended family. We identified this difference as an Event. Then, rather than resisting each other's perspective, they opted to accept what was and work together to find creative ways to honor each other's values and needs. Indeed, merely letting go of resistance can be a solution in itself. For some people, though, this particular difference in values could be a deal breaker, especially when "family" includes previous partners and dysfunctional dynamics.

Following the heart-wrenching attacks of September 11th, 2001, *USA Today* published a poll of Americans' values before and after the event.

Prior to 9/11, Americans rated their values in this order	*After 9/11, Americans rated their values in this order*
1. Career	1. Family
2. Heart	2. Heart
3. Wealth	3. God
4. Health	4. Health
5. Family	5. Country
6. Home	6. Home
7. God	7. Career
8. Country	8. Wealth

Most of us found that day to be a huge wake-up call with regard to what truly mattered. Many questioned their life choices and the way they spent their time. People suddenly recognized that work and wealth were unlikely to be the things that mattered most when their lives and lifestyles were threatened. Family, relationships, and spirituality moved to the top of the list. The problem, of course, was sustaining the reprioritized values without having the skills to do so. As time passed, many people unconsciously slipped back into their old way of prioritizing things—not necessarily because they wanted to but because that is what they knew. People know how to do their jobs because they've been trained. Making relationships work and nurturing one's spiritual life are not as simple—in part because most people haven't been trained in those skills. In light of the importance of these priorities, however, the benefits of doing the work and learning the skills are well worth the effort.

My book *Intellectual Foreplay* (see Resources) is an excellent couple's tool for identifying questions to ask when exploring each other's values. When working with the EROS Equation, having your values clearly identified will help you guide your response options with integrity.

 ## *Brainstorm about Your Personal Values*

Write down each of your values on a separate Post-it Note. That way, you can easily reorder them. Prioritize the list, identifying the ten most important values.

As you do the exercise, consider where you got each value. From your family? Television? Church? A club? Do you really honor each one, or have you just unconsciously listed some without fully embracing them? Be sure that the values you list are truly your own.

After you have identified your values, define what each one means to you.

These are your core values, and they will guide you when making decisions. Keep them consciously in mind and commit yourself to living in alignment with them, allowing them to guide your responses. The results will be greater self-esteem, clarity, focus, and problem-solving ability—and a healthier love life.

The first time I did this exercise, I found myself humming a song during the process. My list included: (1) service to God; (2) having an "attitude of gratitude" and expressing my appreciation; (3) kindness, compassion, and love; (4) honesty, trust, and sincerity; (5) health and strength; (6) personal and spiritual growth; (7) creativity and artistic expression; (8) knowledge and intellectual growth; (9) beauty, peace, and aesthetics; (10) productivity and financial self-sufficiency. Once I finished, I thought about the song that had been going through my head. As I put words to the tune, I realized it was the Camp Fire Girl Law. (Camp Fire Girls is an organization similar to Girl Scouts.) The lyrics went like this: "Worship God, seek beauty, give service, and knowledge pursue. Be trustworthy ever in all that you do. Hold fast onto health and your work glorify, and you will be happy in the Law of Camp Fire."

As I looked down at my journal, I was amazed to see that virtually every one of the values declared in that little song was on my paper. This recognition caused me to wonder whether the values were actually mine or whether they had just been planted in my brain at a very young age. In line with questioning my personal mythology, I took a deep look at each value I had listed. I decided that I truly liked them and wanted them for my own. Even though I chose the values I had learned as a girl, it was by choice rather than through unconscious conditioning.

26 Claim Your Ethics

Live one day at a time, emphasizing ethics rather than rules.

— WAYNE DYER

All of us have a code of ethics or set of rules we live by, but as with our values, we are not always conscious of it. Unconsciously chosen rules often spring from an unexamined personal mythology, and we may find that living by them leads us away from our goals instead of toward them. On the flip side, if rules are instilled in us that we aren't choosing to follow, our sense of integrity may suffer.

When I asked participants in a relationship workshop what rules they lived by, one man raised his hand and said, "Don't get caught"—much to his wife's dismay. Another woman said she had a rule that every marriage should be allowed one major "mistake," or infidelity, per year. Obviously, if you hold these beliefs as your personal, yet possibly unconscious, code of ethics and your partner does not feel the same way, trouble could develop. Having a code of ethics that we have consciously chosen and are committed to can greatly assist us in making choices about how to handle situations and how to treat others. Stated another way, our ethics can help guide our Responses to Events. And discussing your code of ethics with a partner can help both of you gain clarity about your expectations for yourself, each other, and the relationship.

To create a code of ethics that will assist you in your love life, it helps to become aware of the rules you currently operate by, whether consciously or unconsciously. Here are some common rules that may come to mind:

"Honesty is the best policy."

"If you can't say something nice, don't say anything at all."

"Marriages should be monogamous."

"Children are to be seen and not heard."

"The man is the head of the household."

"The woman should not initiate sex."

Keep in mind that although you were exposed to many of these rules growing up, you may not really believe in them, and they may not actually serve you. In fact, some may be obstacles to attaining your goals.

Your code of ethics should work in conjunction with your values, which you explored in the last chapter.

If you are in a relationship, see which rules you have in common with your partner, which rules you might like to adopt from each other's code, and which rules the two of you wish to discard because they don't fit your relationship.

Of course, the Golden Rule—"Do unto others as you would have them do unto you"—is a common rule that many people automatically think of when asked to list their code of ethics. However, it can be a tricky one to live by because the only way it truly works is if the individual has a strong sense of self-esteem—of who he or she really is—and truly knows his or her value. If a person feels undeserving of love and therefore is comfortable being treated horribly, he or she might allow others to mistreat him or her. Consequently, treating others poorly may seem acceptable, when obviously it is not.

Perhaps the Golden Rule should really say, "Do unto others as *they* would have you do unto *them*." We need to treat people the way *they* want to be treated, which is not necessarily the way *we* want to be treated. An example of how this works is that I like to be touched firmly, like a massage stroke, whereas my husband likes to be touched more lightly, like a tickle. If we followed the Golden Rule he would caress me with a feather-light touch and I would use firm strokes on him—and neither of us would be touched the way we prefer.

Some of the rules listed above may just need a little editing to turn them into principles you genuinely embrace:

"Honesty *with thoughtfulness* is the best policy."

"Say what you mean and do what you say."

"Always think about where your words will land before you speak."

"Listen with your heart, not just your ears."

"The thoughts and feelings of every member of the family are important."

When you have defined your values and your personal code of ethics, and when you actively live in alignment with them, you will be living authentically, expressing who you really are in your words, thoughts, and actions. Your Responses to life's Events are far more likely to lead you where you want to go. I guarantee that if you do this, your relationships, which depend on your integrity, will be healthier.

THE INVITATION | *Explore the Rules You Live By*

Make a list of every rule you can think of that you may currently be living by, whether consciously or unconsciously before now.

After you have made your list, examine each rule to see if it is yours or if it was imposed on you by someone else. See if each rule will lead you toward your targets or away from them. Determine whether you are truly committed to abiding by this code of ethics.

You may find you have some rules on your list that you don't really believe in or that haven't been serving you.

Now create a new code of ethics that is made up only of the rules you really believe in. An easy way to test each rule is to ask yourself whether you have broken it or think there is a good chance you will break it. If you're not committed to a rule, don't pretend that you will live by it. Instead, include in your code only those rules you deeply believe in, or create new ones that you are willing to abide by.

27 | The Path of Self-Mastery

> *Incredible change happens in your life when*
> *you decide to take control of what you*
> *do have power over instead of craving*
> *control over what you don't.*
>
> — STEVE MARABOLI

The power of the EROS Equation truly knows no limits. When we take responsibility for how we approach our life circumstances, we realize how powerful we actually are.

Sometimes we get so caught up in thinking that making a relationship last is the most important goal, when in fact there is nothing more important than our own self-mastery. Relationships come and go, people get sick and die, things change. In the end, we have to be able to look back on our lives and know we had integrity in the way we lived—no matter our relationship status.

I once had a client who said, "I can't tell whether my husband is deaf or not listening to me." I apply the EROS Equation to every problem. Essentially she was telling me that the Event was her husband's not hearing her. I asked about her Responses.

"What would you do if your husband were deaf?" She immediately stepped into the option of acceptance (see Chapter 17) and accessed the creativity of her True Nature: "I would be really understanding, helpful, and compassionate. I would make sure he knew I was trying to communicate. I might write him notes or devise another plan to get his attention." She answered from a loving and caring place.

I asked, "What would you do if your husband were not listening to you?" Without hesitation she jumped into the ego response of resistance (see Chapter 16). "I would be angry and hurt. We would get into fights. I would be judgmental and sarcastic." She was clearly walking the path of resistance, which never, ever leads toward a constructive Solution. I said, "Then pretend he is deaf."

You see, it doesn't really matter what is actually true—whether her husband is deaf or not listening. What truly matters is how she shows up with him. If she were to take a deeper look at her responsibility, she may even find that he wasn't listening because of the sarcastic, resistant way she was speaking to him. (I want to make it clear that I'm not saying this couple's communication problems were all the fault of the wife. Remember that the EROS Equation isn't about placing blame. The point is that *she* is the one who had come to me for coaching, not her husband, so we were working on *her* Responses, not his, which were the only thing under her control. If he had been my client, I would have addressed his response options.)

Her resistance, generated from the ego-need for control and/or approval, gave her a heavy dose of the "hards." She became the "bear in the room" and he reacted defensively. The relationship had taken take the path that would lead away from the target of love. Ego says, "It isn't my fault; it is his/hers." Ego asks, "Why am I the one who has to do the work when he/she is the one who…?" My reply is, "Because you are the one who wants to be happy more than right. Although he/she may be the one who did something to harm you, you are the one in relationship with him/her. You are not a victim. Let's see how you can respond differently to create a different result."

People often think I am suggesting they just "deal with it"—as in "put up with it." And I *am* suggesting that you deal with it, but not from a place of resistance and resentment. Rather, when you access your True Nature you are better equipped to deal with any situation creatively, and you stand a chance of actually solving the problem.

A labyrinth with only one path to the center, as illustrated in Chapter 19, is a great metaphor for your True Nature in the midst of chaos. However, finding the right Response in the EROS Equation may seem a bit more like being in a maze with multiple possible paths. Some response options will lead to a dead end, others may lead to a trap, and others will lead you more deeply into the morass. Yet if you take a moment to contemplate your choices, you will see that there is always a route that is a healthier option, a "higher path." It is the one that, regardless of the outcome, allows you to retain self-respect and a sense of integrity. No choice you make is a failure if you remain self-observant and learn what works and what doesn't. Allow your values and ethics to guide you into making the best decisions. This is the path of responsibility rather than blame. This is the path of self-mastery.

I once traveled to India, where I had the honor of sitting in the presence of a holy man. As I sat across from him, I became acutely aware that he knew everything about me. He didn't say so, but I knew that he knew about every decision I had made— every indiscretion and misdeed as well as every wise choice. All I felt from him while I perceived him silently reviewing my life's choices was unconditional love and compassion. I, however, squirmed in his presence under the weight of my own self-judgment.

I came to the conclusion that "Judgment Day" is not when God judges and punishes or rewards us, but rather when we stand in the presence of unconditional love and judge ourselves. In this presence, the "reward" or "punishment" is whether we feel worthy or unworthy of such compassion, understanding, and love. I vowed then and there that when I had the opportunity to again sit face to face with a holy presence I would be able to do so without squirming. I vowed to be certain that my choices— my Responses—from that moment forward were in alignment with who I *really* am. I vowed to make my own self-mastery and integrity my highest priorities. Then I found myself wondering if perhaps we *are* in this presence all the time.

 *Practice Self-Awareness*

Imagine what it is like to be in a relationship with you. What is it like to love you? What is it like to eat a meal with you? Talk to you? Listen to you? What is it like to make love with you, or to want to? What is it like to live with you? Self-awareness will lead to understanding, which is the first step to change. If you like being with you, notice it. If not, make some new choices.

PART EIGHT

MANAGING EMOTIONS
AND CHANGE

I don't want to be at the mercy of my emotions.
I want to use them, to enjoy them, and to dominate them.
— OSCAR WILDE

The goal to make wise choices and carefully considered responses is a good one, but the road to Hell is paved with good intentions, as they say. Emotions, particularly those generated from the ego, can cloud our decision-making ability. When we are jealous, hurt, afraid, or angry, we need an extra dose of mindfulness to bring us in off the ledge of relationship destruction.

The following chapters will help you improve your ability to translate the protective emotional messages of the ego into powerful decisions. They will also guide you to understand the process of change—knowing when to give up and when to persevere.

28 The Beauty of Fear

> *Courage is not the absence of fear, but*
> *rather the judgment that something else is more*
> *important than fear.*
> — AMBROSE REDMOON

Most of us have come to look at fear as a sign saying, "Turn back, you fool!" When fear arises in a relationship it tends to dictate how we behave. We begin to imagine events that may or may not happen and attribute thoughts to people they may or may not be thinking.

It can be hard to distinguish between fear and intuition. Both are gifts meant to protect us or something we cherish—our lives, our families, our relationships. The only way I know to tell the two apart is to pay close attention to what you are feeling and to what thoughts and images arise. Then inquire whether the images empower you to take an action step, as if meant to help you protect yourself, or whether they paralyze you with anxiety, jealousy, or rage. Intuition is generated from your spirit, your heart—your authentic self. Fear is generated from ego, from your personality. My experience is that intuition is proactive and purposeful. It makes us wiser and stronger. It does not cause us to become unreasonable and judgmental, nor does it make us want to inflict pain or harm others. Intuition offers us information we can use to strengthen and protect ourselves or someone else. Intuition offers the truth, and even if painful the truth will make you more authentic and more capable.

With a little awareness, you can transform fear into something that serves you rather than hinders you. When you feel fear, it is an excellent opportunity to self-observe and self-inquire to see what meaning you are making out of the situation. You may have heard fear defined as "**f**antasized **e**xperiences **a**ppearing **r**eal." It's one of those clichés that tend to be accurate. Most of the time when we feel fear, the thing we are afraid of isn't really happening; we are only concerned that it will happen. Yet we behave as if it were happening. Giving our fears too much credence is a slippery slope that can lead toward the very thing we don't want.

It can be helpful to remember that fear is an ego-driven emotion and is, yet again, trying to protect us. As we discussed in Part Three, you need to recognize the ego's attempts to protect you, listen to it, but not necessarily believe it at face value. If indeed there is a good reason to be afraid or a protective action to be taken, beautiful! Fear may have just saved your life. If not, take a peek underneath your fear. Think of fear as a big boulder marking where a treasure is hidden. Instead of turning back or running away when you encounter the "fear boulder," you have the opportunity to discover something important, something that matters to you. Fear reveals to you that which you cherish and want to protect. Take a moment to look under the fear boulder. Use self-inquiry to dig, and determine what the treasure is.

For example, if you are afraid that your partner is going to cheat on you, your fear becomes the Event and you may react as if it were true. If you give too much credence to your fear, you will go into resistance and respond with some combination of suspicion, anger, distrust, accusation, and emotional withdrawal. You may withhold intimacy. You may call your partner a thousand times to check up on him or her, and snoop through e-mails or cell phone numbers in search of evidence. Your behaviors may actually create the outcome you fear by pushing your partner away from you.

If instead you were to look under the fear boulder to discover something about yourself, you would see that the reason you are afraid is because you treasure the relationship with your partner. If you honor your relationship from the perspective of what you cherish instead of what you fear, then your behaviors will be more kind, loving, trusting, accepting, and intimate. This Response is more likely to cause your partner to cherish the relationship, too.

Taking these steps is the path of self-mastery. You may find yourself thinking it is all "too much work" or "too hard." Or you may be afraid that if you transcend the ego, you will fall into an abyss of nothingness. Look underneath those fears, too. You will likely see that the treasure of real, lasting love and true joy is hiding there. What lies beneath the ego is a brilliant being capable of great work, great love, and great relationships.

Reinterpret the ego's messages, and make the choice to align with your soul. Rather than running from fear—or fearing it—allow it to be the signpost to your greatest treasures.

THE INVITATION | Look for the Treasure Beneath Your Fears

Whenever you feel fear, take a deep breath and give yourself a few minutes to self-inquire. What are you afraid of? Is it happening now? What is the story you are telling yourself or the meaning you are making that is causing you concern? What is hidden beneath your fear that you love and cherish and want to protect? How would you behave differently if you honored what you love instead of what you fear? What do you think the outcome would be if you aligned your actions with the Solution you want?

29 | *Understanding the Mountain of Emotions*

> *Don't hold on to anger, hurt, or pain. They steal your energy and keep you from love.*
> — LEO BUSCAGLIA

Every relationship, whether at work, at home, or with a stranger, has the ability to evoke anger. When an Event happens and we resist what is, we may express our anger, hoping to bring about a change in the other person or the situation. Unfortunately, it doesn't exactly work like that.

When we feel anger, to most of us it feels like an isolated emotion, one that exists by itself. We think we are simply angry. We express our anger and request an agreement for change. Then the other person gets defensive and expresses their anger. Fear and hurt get mixed in from the meaning we make based on our personal mythology. Then the interaction spirals out of control and we get stuck in these emotions. This is a nearly impossible platform upon which to build agreements for change and healthy relationships.

Just like the fear boulder, anger lets us know that something else is going on—if we take the time to look. When we become aware of our feelings—particularly the ego-generated emotions that don't feel good, like anger, hurt, fear, jealousy, frustration, or anxiety—and stop to inquire by looking deeper into them, we can use them to guide us back to love.

When we feel **anger** or one of its variations—frustration, irritation, annoyance, or resentment—it is like a flag on top of a mountain of other emotions. It doesn't exist by itself. Several other emotions are also affecting us.

Directly under the anger lies **hurt.** When we are mad at someone, we also feel hurt in some way by them or the situation. Sometimes the hurt is due to what the other person actually did; sometimes it is due to the meaning we made out of the behavior—a meaning that may not be accurate at all.

Underneath the hurt is **fear.** We are afraid of losing the relationship, afraid of what others will think of us, afraid that we will continue to be hurt, afraid that we will never be able to trust again, afraid that we are being made to look foolish, and on and on. None of which may be true. Ultimately, we are afraid of losing control or losing approval. Our need for control is embedded in anger, and our need for approval in hurt. Both are hiding in our fears.

Underneath the fear lies **responsibility**: recognition of or remorse over our part in the situation. It is rare to encounter a conflict or circumstance for which we do not have some responsibility. Even if it is simply being in the wrong place at the wrong time, the way we reacted to something that happened, or the story we made up about it, if we look closely we can usually see our part in the problem. When expressing the whole truth of our feelings, it is very empowering to admit to ourselves (and to let others know) what we are sorry for and what we could have done differently. Remember, our feelings are the result of something we thought (our Response to an Event). If you are feeling angry, hurt, and fearful, taking responsibility for your thoughts can change the way you feel. It is in our response-ability that the power to heal and change exists. As I said before, recognizing our responsibility neutralizes the ego magnet and can bring us back into balance.

When we look beneath our responsibility in a situation, we arrive at a sense of **understanding.** There is usually something that we know is affecting the other person—maybe a hard day at work or memories of a rotten childhood or hormones or stress or illness. In other words, when we transcend our ego and drop our guards of defense and resistance for a moment, we can feel some compassion for what the other person is experiencing. From a place of understanding, we may see the other person's perspective and possibly even their innocence, or why they did what they did. Or we uncover the misunderstanding that contributed to the situation. When we achieve a sense of understanding and compassion, we are far better equipped to forgive. "Forgiveness" comes from a root word that means "to give." When we take the time to look at the situation from our heart, with compassion and understanding, instead of from our ego, what really matters and what does not begin to become clear. We remove the ego blocks and restore the ability to give and receive love.

Beneath understanding and forgiveness is what we **want.** We want to be treated fairly, we want a loving relationship—or we may want out. We need to know where we are trying to go in order to figure out how to get there. This is why identifying your target, as discussed in Part Six, or the Solution you want to create, covered in Part Four, is so important.

Underneath what we want is **appreciation, love,** or **acknowledgment.** Regardless of the fact that we're feeling all these emotions, there are still things we appreciate about the other person. Underneath the mountain of emotions, love still exists. In fact, in some cases we wouldn't even feel anger if the other person didn't matter so much to us. The love is easier to see when we're dealing with partners or family members than it is with total strangers, but even when we don't know the person we are angry at, on the soul level we care about him or her as a human being. With our loved ones, it is much easier to recognize and express what we love and appreciate about them. **The bottom line is love.**

Anger, hurt, and fear are ego-generated emotions designed to protect us. The goal isn't to ignore them, but nor is it to dive into them without exploring the total truth and our responsibility in things. Once we acknowledge our part in our circumstances, we shift into accessing powerful, spirit-generated possibilities for managing the situation, and we begin to see creative response options. And the other person often starts listening once they know we aren't merely blaming them for our emotions.

One woman told me she wanted to leave her husband, so I guided her through the layers of anger. Essentially she said, "I'm angry that he is always working. I feel like I'm raising the kids alone. I am hurt that he doesn't place more priority on spending time with me. I'm afraid that we are going to grow farther apart and eventually I will want the attention of other men. I am sorry that I haven't always been a pleasant person to come home to. I realize that I am often unwelcoming and judgmental. I understand that work may be a preferable place to be and that it must be frustrating to work so hard to support the family and have me seem so unappreciative. What I want is to have a fun, loving, intimate relationship again. What I appreciate and love about him is the fact that he is fun to be with." Clearly, this is a far cry from "I want a divorce," yet she arrived there in a mere eight sentences.

When we take the time to inquire into all the feelings we are experiencing, sometimes we find that the original event we were reacting to isn't even the real issue that needs addressing. When we dive into the total truth of our emotions, we often reveal a deeper truth.

Investigate the Total Truth*

When you encounter a conflict, think through your answers to the sentence stems that follow (or write them in a journal), fully expressing the total truth of your emotions. Sometimes just thinking through your emotions will move you to resolution, and you will have no need to discuss the matter with your partner. You may be able to gain understanding, take responsibility, achieve forgiveness, and let go of anger simply by becoming aware of all that you are feeling and the meaning you have made. If a discussion and agreement are necessary, when you are ready, share the whole truth of your feelings with your partner. Ask him or her to listen to all of your emotions before responding, and encourage him or her to use the same format as you listen.

This tool is also great for letting go of built-up emotion over past relationships, or clearing up unfinished business with people who have passed away or with whom you are no longer in contact.

* Adapted from the teachings of Jack Canfield, who learned the exercise from John Gray and Barbara DeAngelis.

Here are the sentence stems for you to complete:

I felt angry when...

I was hurt that...

I am afraid that...

I am sorry for...

I understand that...

What I want is...

What I appreciate or love you about you is...

What I'd like to agree to is...

After you have transcended the need for approval and control, and you and your partner have expressed the full range of your feelings—and have listened to each other—see if you can come to an agreement. When we express our full range of emotions—anger, hurt, fear, responsibility, understanding, forgiveness, want, and love—we can then begin the process of negotiation and agreement, if it is needed. Remember, however, that negotiation is still a request for the Event to change and may or may not work (refer to Chapter 15). Your power always lies in your ability to explore creative options for your behavior. Other people will respond differently to you when you show up differently.

Remember, love and anger exist simultaneously. Be sure when you are expressing the anger that your love is also shining through.

30 *One Hundred Percent Response-Ability*

> *You may believe that you are responsible for what you do, but not for what you think. The truth is that you are responsible for what you think, because it is only at this level that you can exercise choice. What you do comes from what you think.*
>
> — MARIANNE WILLIAMSON

Your happiness is 100 percent up to you. When you blame your relationship, job, school, sweetheart, or any other person for your reality, you are cheating yourself out of your happiness.

When you think you have to do something or stay in a situation that isn't good for you, I invite you to be more creative in your solution search and in your thinking. We always have choices either about what we are doing or about how we think and feel about what we are doing. If you truly *have* to do whatever it is, how can you reframe it or change the way you see it so it no longer causes you so much pain?

When you choose to do something (even if your only reason is to avoid the consequences of not doing it) and you resist doing it, you are only causing suffering for yourself—and usually for others. Responses that harm others are never in alignment with who you really are and will never, ultimately, lead to a Solution. I encourage you to shift into acceptance. It will set you free.

Let's examine what 100 percent responsibility would look like in a real-life situation. It's not feasible to list every possible Event/Response scenario here, but I can lead you through a typical one so you can see the process in action. Regardless of what your Events are, you always have powerful response options. Let me remind you that any situation that you approach with your ego magnets of approval and control activated is going to evoke resistance in the other person, even if you offer what seems like a kind, reasonable Response. The ego magnet can be tangibly felt, even if the words or actions are pleasant. **Always do the work of self-mastery first** to achieve the best results. The Essential Life and Love Skills (Part Six) provide a practice for self-mastery.

Most of us think when we are mastering the Response in the EROS Equation that only what we say and do it is relevant. For the most part, we can see our responsibility for the impact of our words and actions on the Outcome. But let's take a look at the power of thoughts and your responsibility over them. In fact, what we choose to think is what charges or defuses the ego magnets. For instance, in the realm of intimacy, thoughts are critical in terms of what you are thinking about your partner, what you are thinking about yourself, and what you are thinking your partner is thinking about you. It sounds confusing because it can be. Our thoughts have the power to turn a beautiful moment into a horrendous one, or vice versa.

Imagine the Event is that your partner is preparing for a romantic evening and lights a candle. The candle causes you to think about whether you have paid the electrical bill yet. Suddenly you are totally preoccupied with paying bills, and the romantic mood quickly disappears. What you were thinking about totally changed the mood, and undoubtedly the Outcome, of the evening. Notice the lack of alignment with the target of a harmonious relationship.

Imagine that your partner is preparing for a romantic evening and you start thinking, *Again? He (or she) only acts this way when he wants sex. I'm sick and tired of having to respond every time he....* The romantic opportunity is now contaminated with what you are thinking about your partner. Notice the need for control.

Imagine that your partner is preparing for a romantic evening and places her (or his) hand around your waist. You start wondering if she can feel how much weight you've gained. You start to be uncomfortable with your partner's touches and attention because you are thinking about having to get naked in front of her. Then you start thinking about how out of shape you have become and how uncomfortable you are with your body.

The romantic mood is severely damaged because of what you are thinking about yourself. Notice the need for approval.

Imagine that your partner is preparing for a romantic evening and glances over at you and smiles sweetly. Then you notice that his (or her) eyes pass over the pile of clothes in the corner of the room, which haven't yet made it to the laundry hamper. You start thinking that he is wondering what you did all day. You guess, *Does he think I was watching TV? He must think I'm lazy. Doesn't he know how much I do? How dare he!* Suddenly you are mad and fighting with your spouse instead of sharing a romantic evening— all because of a story you made up in your head about what you thought your spouse was thinking about you. All he may have really been thinking was how much he was looking forward to what he thought was about to come next. Notice the meaning that is being made, a story that may not even be true.

Notice that in every one of these scenarios the event was the same: Your partner was preparing for a romantic evening. In terms of the EROS Equation, your Response to the Event—in this case, in the form of thoughts—is what created the different outcomes, none of which were in alignment with the goal of having a healthy, loving relationship.

You can change what you think, but to do so you have to become aware of your thoughts and of what they are doing to you (instead of blaming your partner). This requires practicing self-observation, noticing your self-talk, transcending the ego-needs for approval and control, and choosing Responses in alignment with your goal for the relationship (or evening).

Imagine that your partner is preparing for a romantic evening. Your first thought is that you aren't in the mood or you have too much to do. If you go ahead and make love from your need for approval, you will be resentful and it will be an unpleasant exchange. Even though sex will have taken place, intimacy will not have. Take a deep breath, transcend your ego-need for approval and control, drop into your heart and into your authenticity. See if you can make the decision from authenticity instead of ego. It may be that in the present moment, making your partner happy is absolutely in alignment with your big-picture goal of having a loving, harmonious relationship. If so, let go of resistance, switch into acceptance, and enjoy an intimate exchange with your partner.

If, in the present moment, you know that you cannot authentically make love with your partner for whatever real reason (a deadline, an illness, lack of time, etc.), again, take a deep breath. Transcend the need for approval and control, and move into the present moment. Then find another response in alignment with a loving, harmonious relationship. Lovingly set a date for when you would like to have an intimate encounter so you aren't triggering his/her need for approval, and take responsibility for following through at that time, or encourage your partner to take care of him- or herself while you assist or watch—or not. Or...

what other options do you have to honor both your relationship and your own needs? Be creative, communicative, and appreciative.

Every choice has an outcome or consequence. When we take responsibility for our choices, we are no longer victims.

Notice Your Thoughts and Shift into Gratitude

Notice when your thoughts shift into subtle or not-so-subtle resistance to the tasks you've committed to. Remind yourself that each of them relates to a goal you've adopted—whether it's making love to keep your marriage healthy, or paying taxes to be compliant, or going to work to make money, or cleaning house for your sanity, or exercising to stay fit, or caring for an elderly or sick relative because you love them. Even though each of these behaviors relates to one of your desired aims, you may still find yourself resisting (complaining about) them from time to time.

When you find this happening, shift your attention to what you love or appreciate about your partner, your job, your family. Notice what your loved ones and coworkers do well. Notice the same thing about yourself, and practice describing the good qualities about yourself. Every time you observe yourself running a judgmental banter tape in your head (or from your mouth), consciously notice and shift your attention to the positive. Think-

ing negatively about everything or everyone is just a habit. With a little consciousness and attention, the habit can be broken.

Think like a miner. When a miner goes into a gold mine, he has to remove tons and tons of dirt and rock to find a single nugget of gold, but a miner never goes into the mine looking for the dirt. You can look for the dirt or you can look for the gold in yourself and others. It all depends on what you want to find. It is your choice.

31 Change the Moment, Change the Relationship

> *There are three constants in life...*
> *change, choice, and principles.*
> — STEVEN COVEY

We can't go into a relationship expecting to change the other person, but we should expect that they will change. The difference is in *who* drives the change. We cannot make our partner change, but the forces of nature as well as their own impetus will cause them to change. Their body will change. Their hormones will change. Their libido will change. Their weight may change. Their health may change. Their physical appearance may change. Their friendships may change. Their careers may change. Their hobbies may change. Their athletic activities may change. Their level of alcohol consumption may change. Their confidence and self-esteem may change. Their minds may even change. And they will change the way they behave in response to the way we behave toward them. So what is it exactly that we expect to stay the same?

Then there is the relationship itself, which will change as a separate entity from either partner. Frequency of "date nights" may change. Level of financial comfort may change. Where you live may change. Time available for recreation may change. Family support may change. Number of family members may change. Children (who are also ever-changing) will change the relationship. More children will change it even more. Children growing up and moving out of the home will change the relationship. The loss of family members will change the dynamics again. Sexual frequency and ability may change. Skills for problem solving and communication may change. How you spend your time together and how much time you spend together may change. Retirement will change things again. So what is it exactly that we expect to stay the same?

The love is probably what we want to stay the same, but even the expression and experience of love changes. Although the core essence of true love is unchanging, as it filters through our egos it appears to change as our access to it changes. As I've said already, love doesn't go away but it can get blocked with ego—the experience of it ebbs and flows. Love can deepen over time, moving from infatuation to a greater sense of security. Love can be more or less passionate. Love can be conditional or unconditional. Love can be expressed or withheld. Love can be given and not received. The intensity of the love in a relationship can shift, as can the intimacy. If we want to be successful in our relationships (and in our lives), we have to become comfortable with change—both responding to it (the Event) when it happens, and creating it (the Solution) when needed.

This is where all the skills we have discussed in this book become a necessity. If we want to create change in a relationship, we must create change in ourselves. Change requires our ability to "accept what is" and be flexible in responding to the issues of the present moment rather than reacting to our memory of issues from the past or our fear of possible issues in the future. As we become more flexible and creative in our responses, we create more powerful results.

When we first begin changing the way we are, the way we do things, and the way we respond to events, it can seem overwhelming. Sometimes our momentary lapses in judgment or memory make change feel impossible. We may have it mastered one day, and the next, if we're underfed or overtired or stressed, we may feel like we are never going to get our responses right.

As I pointed out in Part Three, the ego has a really hard time with commitment. When you decide you are going to do something differently forever, the ego often rebels. It will serve you to do your best to remember that the only thing you have any control over is how you choose to behave in the moment. When one moment doesn't go well, you have the next moment to take a deep breath, recalibrate, and start again.

It is not possible to change tomorrow or the next day, and certainly not "forever." However, every time you master a moment and realign with your goals, and then master the next moment, they string together into eternity and the future has been changed—one moment at a time. Imagine that "happily ever after" is not the goal of a relationship, but rather "happily right now."

Refer one more time to the image of the labyrinth on page 113. Find the entrance at the bottom of the illustration, and with your eyes follow the path into the labyrinth. Shortly after the first 180-degree turn, the path arrives at a spot next to the center. It is so easy at that point to think, *Look at that. I am almost there!* Then the path continues through the entire labyrinth until you find yourself next to the entrance again. About that time you might think, *I'm never going to get there. I'm right back where I started!* The temptation to give up and step out of the labyrinth can be overwhelming. Yet if you follow the path through just one more 180-degree turn, you will soon reach your destination. What a fitting metaphor for how change happens.

As you apply the EROS Equation in your relationships—and your life—you may enjoy a few immediate successes that give you hope and confidence. Then you may find yourself spiraling deeper into the process, feeling as if you are lost. Stay true to the path of your authenticity, values, and integrity. Even when it feels like you should give up, pick yourself up, refer to the Six Essential Life and Love Skills, and choose your Responses carefully. I guarantee that if you persevere, the journey will prove worth your effort. And it will get easier!

THE INVITATION | Don't Give Up. Give *UP*!

In the movie Groundhog Day, *the character played by Bill Murray finds himself waking up on the same day over and over again. Every morning he is faced with the exact same set of Events, if you will. Every day is Groundhog Day in Punxsutawney, and all the people he interacts with are exactly the same. The only thing that ever changes is how he responds to the Events (and people) and thus how they respond to him. This is the perfect example of the EROS Equation at work. As long as his responses are based in ego—arrogant, unkind, or selfish—he remains in the time loop. It is not until he aligns his choices with love, compassion, and kindness that he is allowed to move forward in time and to build a healthy relationship. If you have not seen this movie, I encourage you to watch it with EROS in mind.*

Instead of "giving up" and surrendering when you find yourself in resistance, or when your choices have yet again led you away from your target, "give UP" to your higher self. When you catch yourself in the depths of despair or engaging in old habits, it is as if you have fallen into a deep, dark pit that you vowed never to fall into again. Instead of taking up residence in the hole, pull out the tools that reside in your heart and use them to climb out. Every time you successfully pull yourself up and out of the pit of unconsciousness, the hole will get shallower. It is as if you knock debris off the sides as you climb, filling in the hole a bit each time. Eventually, there will be no pit; it will be more like a little pothole that you stumble over from time to time. You will be able to catch yourself quickly, regain balance, and step back onto the path that leads to harmonious relationships.

PART NINE

THE SOUL-UTION

One evening, an elderly Cherokee brave told his grandson about a battle
that goes on inside people. He said, "My son, the battle is between two
'wolves' inside us all. One is evil. It is anger, envy, jealousy, sorrow,
regret, greed, arrogance, self-pity, guilt, resentment, inferiority, lies,
false pride, superiority, and ego. The other is good. It is joy, peace,
love, hope, serenity, humility, kindness, benevolence, empathy,
generosity, truth, compassion, and faith."
The grandson thought about it for a minute and then asked,
"Grandfather, which wolf wins?"
His grandfather replied, "The one that you feed."
— OLD CHEROKEE TALE

We all have a choice in every moment about how we show up in
our relationships and our world. It only takes a split second to
make a choice that can save your life or destroy it, make your relationships falter or thrive. One choice—during the span of one
breath—can make all the difference.

32 Train Your Brain to Start with Heart

> *Educating the mind without educating the heart is no education at all.*
> — ARISTOTLE

If I had to sum up all the material in this book in one sentence, it would be: "Train your brain to start with heart, rather than ego." When you start with your heart, remembering your goal of creating a healthy, harmonious relationship, you can use your head to assist you. The EROS Equation provides a powerful formula for using your head and your heart together in the realm of love.

Many of us move through life asleep to who we really are, operating unconsciously from ego. Every now and then we have a conscious, aware moment or an experience of authenticity. If we happen to be with someone else, we may share the moment heart to heart. But we usually quickly dismiss it as "nothing," pretend it didn't happen, or fall back to sleep. Forgetting who we really are, we get lulled back into bad habits, resistance, judgment, posses-siveness, and jealousy.

Since nearly everyone is operating at the same level of (un) consciousness, much of our entertainment reinforces this mindless programming. We don't even know that our choices are the reason why our relationships aren't working. We think it is someone else. We may even think it is the random arrows of Eros, the god of love, that account for the phenomenon of "he loves me, she loves me not" we so often experience in our lives.

The truth is we are not victims of anyone else, including the god of love. The EROS Equation is the antidote to all these external forces, and when you apply it to every life experience, every relationship, you will discover your power to love and be loved. When you use the Essential Life and Love Skills, you be-come equipped to drop into your True Nature, where you can listen with your heart for the deeper meaning behind every in-teraction and every emotion.

Simply make it your intention to regularly observe your ego magnets at work and take responsibility for what you are attract-ing into your life. That is the key to creating real-ationships based in true love instead of battleships anchored in the ego-need for approval or control. When you do this, you will turn the journey of love around. Instead of being mostly asleep and enjoying rare moments of wakefulness, you will remain awake with perhaps an occasional moment of lack of consciousness.

Even then you will have the skills and tools required to wake yourself right back up.

As you walk your heart path, you will encourage and inspire others to do the same. When you monitor your own Responses, people will respond differently to you. When you remember who you really are, you will also remember who they really are. That is how change happens.

When you learn to start with heart, you will quickly clear the obstacles between yourself and love.

THE INVITATION | Find the Blessing

It is my sincere belief that the world is out to do us good and that our job is to find the good in everything that happens. Often this just requires some time and a different perspective. In each situation, when you find yourself resisting someone or something, if you simply stop and contemplate the question "How is this a blessing to me?" you will likely find an answer. This inquiry can quickly move you into acceptance and gratitude. Regardless of whether or not the Event is a direct blessing, it will either result in a blessing of some sort or provide you with the opportunity to respond in such a way that you become stronger, wiser, more creative, or more intuitive. There is always a blessing.

I invite you to look upon your challenges and ask, How is this a blessing to me? What did I learn? How has this strengthened me? Who has this brought into my life? What did this event lead to? What positive qualities does this situation exercise in me?

Ask the same questions about the very thing your sweetheart, spouse, or family member does that bothers you. Sit in inquiry for a few minutes, and I am confident you will find at least one answer.

33 *Simply a Choice*

> *Put your heart, mind, and soul into even your smallest acts. This is the secret of success.*
> — SWAMI SIVANANDA

While the application of the EROS Equation is perfect for love, the power of its use is not limited to romantic relationships. The formula's potency is available to improve every aspect of our lives.

We are not bodies with a soul; we are souls with a body. We have gotten this concept completely backward to the extent that we have locked our souls deep within us, hidden under a thick layer of "clay." It may seem as though we have thrown away the key, but in truth we have just misplaced it. Much like Rapunzel in the tower hoping someone notices her or hears her calls for help, our souls are constantly trying to get our attention, to wake us up and get us to live our lives more powerfully and lovingly.

The EROS Equation outlines a way to bring our soul—our spirit, our authenticity, our strengths—not only into our relationships but also into the workplace, into our homes, and into our communities. We will immediately know whether or not our Responses are working by the Outcomes we experience. Life gives us clear and immediate feedback.

I own and operate a beautiful garden on Maui called the Sacred Garden. As funny as it sounds, plants have become my teachers. When a plant needs something, it tells you by showing signs of distress—it wilts, or turns brown, or loses its leaves. Our relationships and our lives do the same thing. Our relationships begin to wilt when we stop being mindful of them—when our responses are not nourishing or when there is too much "heat" or too much "cold." Our lives give us signs when things are not working; we start to experience conflicts or stress or boredom. Our body lets us know when we haven't been taking care of it. Weight issues, pain, depression, skin conditions, and illness are all signs that something needs to change. Everywhere you look, your life is speaking to you.

If you are experiencing drama, conflict, or a case of the "hards," try a new Response—toward a loved one, a coworker, a boss, a neighbor. If you are out of shape, depressed, broke, unfulfilled, or lonely, change the way you are doing things. If you want to be happy, healthy, or in love, it may be tempting to think, "I'll be happy when [fill in the blank] changes"—for example, your partner, society, the government. But that mindset won't get you where you want to go. If you want to create a new, healthier experience, explore new, healthier Responses to the people and Events around you.

If you look around, you will see that 99.9 percent of us first try to get other people to change (negotiation). When that doesn't work we blame the other person or the situation and resort to unskilled and unconscious methods of bringing about change based on our egos (resistance). Or, we leave, figuring the grass must be greener on the other side of the fence (get out). We seek a new partner, a new job, a new whatever. When the ego-needs of approval and control get triggered, we start the whole cycle over again. We need to stop this insanity. We need to make new choices. When the grass looks greener on the other side of the fence, I invite you to water your lawn. Re-examine the tools in this book and practice them.

Rather than being a victim of the "arrows" shot into your relationships by external forces, become the archer of your own love life. When an archer shoots an arrow that misses its target, she doesn't say, "That is where the target should have been," or, "That is just where arrows land." Rather, she picks up a new arrow, re-aims, and shoots again. The skilled archer practices until she is able to hit her intended target. That's how the EROS Equation operates.

Take some time to consider your targets. What lifestyle do you want? What quality of relationships are you aiming for? What kind of person do you want to be? What characteristics do you admire? When something happens or someone does something you don't like, identify the Event. Determine what actually happened (rather than the meaning you made out of it). This will help you to identify what you can't change while also recognizing your part—your response-ability—which is where you have power. Then, aim your Responses toward the target of loving and harmonious relationships. If one Response falls short, evaluate the situation, recalibrate to your authenticity, reset your intentions, aim anew for your target, and take action again.

This brings us right back to where the book started, with the Serenity Prayer:

Grant me the serenity to accept the things I cannot change,
the courage to change the things I can,
and the wisdom to know the difference.

You could say that we've changed the second part to read: "…the courage *and the tools* to change the things I can." You now have those tools in your tool belt. The ability to use them comes down to your choice to respond in alignment with who you are and what you want.

We always have a choice: to honor ego or to honor love.

♥THE INVITATION | *Make the Choice*

It may seem like there are many steps to making the EROS Equation work. Once you become familiar with them, however, they can all happen simultaneously, in the space of one breath. Experiment with realigning with your authenticity. Breathe. Choose how you want to show up. Breathe again. It is amazing how different the world looks when you look at the world differently.

It is my sincere belief that you have within you all the abilities, strengths, and resources to create Soul-utions. I invite you to look within and ask yourself:

Are you going to respond with fear or love?

*

Are you going to respond with despair or hope?

*

Are you going to respond with doubt or faith?

*

Are you going to respond with apathy or growth?

*

Are you going to respond with unhappiness or joy?

*

Are you going to respond with deception or honesty?

*

Are you going to respond with anger or compassion?

*

Are you going to respond with resistance or acceptance?

*

Are you going to respond with complacency or commitment?

*

Are you going to respond with resentment or forgiveness?

*

Are you going to respond with the "hards" or the "softs"?

*

Are you going to respond with ego or spirit?

*

The choice is yours.

You are the Soul-ution to the EROS Equation.

Resources

RECOMMENDED READING

Capacchione, Lucia. *The Power of Your Other Hand: A Course in Channeling the Inner Wisdom of the Right Brain.* Pompton Plains, NJ: New Page Books, 2000.

Comaroto, Maryanne. *Hindsight: What You Need to Know Before You Drop Your Drawers.* Greenbrae, CA: Bridge the Gap Publishing, 2009.

Dwoskin, Hale. *The Sedona Method: Your Key to Lasting Happiness, Success, Peace and Emotional Well-Being.* Minnetonka, MN: Sedona Press, 2003.

Katie, Byron. *Loving What Is: Four Questions That Can Change Your Life.* New York: Harmony Books, 2003.

Tolle, Eckhart. *A New Earth: Awakening to Your Life's Purpose,* New York: Penguin Books, 2008.

EVE ESCHNER HOGAN'S BOOKS

How to Love Your Marriage: Making Your Closest Relationship Work. Alameda, CA: Hunter House Publishers, 2005.

Intellectual Foreplay: Questions for Lovers and Lovers to Be. Alameda, CA: Hunter House Publishers, 2000.

Virtual Foreplay: Making Your Online Relationship a Real-Life Success. Alameda, CA: Hunter House Publishers, 2001.

Way of the Winding Path: A Map for the Labyrinth of Life. Ashland, OR: White Cloud Press, 2003.

Rings of Truth by Jim Britt with Eve Eschner Hogan. Deerfield Beach, FL: Health Communications, Inc., 1999.

FOR INFORMATION ABOUT EVE HOGAN'S BOOKS AND EVENTS
www.EveHogan.com
Eve's Blog, Real Love, for *Spirituality and Health Magazine*
http://spiritualityhealth.com/blogs/eve-hogan

FOR INFORMATION ON EVE'S HEART PATH JOURNEYS (RETREATS ON MAUI)
www.SacredMauiRetreats.com

FOR INFORMATION ON THE SACRED GARDEN ON MAUI
www.SacredGardenMaui.com

Six Essential Life Skills

When we are in our heads, we are cut off from our hearts, but when we are in our hearts, we can use our heads. These Essential Life Skills allow us to align *who we really are* and *what we want* with *how we show up* (our actions)—making them one and the same. When we are able to do this, we become immensely powerful, are able to reach our goals, and are able to experience peace, even in the midst of chaos.

1. REMEMBER WHO YOU REALLY ARE— OR WHO YOU WANT TO BE

Remember who you really are or visualize, imagine, discover, or invite that aspect of yourself to be revealed. Look to small children. All the beautiful qualities they possess, we possess, too: enthusiasm, joy, energy, creativity, imagination, curiosity, playfulness, honesty, and authentic self-expression. None of these qualities go away as we grow up, access simply gets blocked. By remembering who you really are or simply starting to look, you forge the path to your heart.

2. IDENTIFY YOUR TARGET—CONSIDER WHAT YOU WANT TO CREATE....

Do you want a harmonious relationship, a healthy body, a successful business, a family, self-esteem, or confidence? In order to get what you want, you need to know where you are aiming.

3. SELF-OBSERVE

Practice self-observation in every moment of every day. Notice what you are doing, saying, and feeling with each step, each word, each thought, and each action. Then ask yourself, "Does this serve me? Does this diminish or enhance the obstacles to my goals?" If your choices do not serve you or are not in alignment with who you really are, then it is time to make new choices. Self-observation leads to self-awareness. Self-awareness allows you the opportunity to make choices. The ability to choose those actions that serve you over those that don't makes you powerful. In order to get where you want to go, you need to know where you currently are in every given moment.

4. MAKE THE CHOICE TO LET GO, TO TRANSCEND THE EGO

As you encounter the behaviors, thoughts, and words that are not serving you, that are blocking access to your heart, take a deep breath and make the choice to let them go. Breathe and let go. You will find that ego is always what blocks our access to love, creativity, and true power. Ironically, your *need* for love and your *need* to be loved are blocking your ability to *be* loving and to *be* loved. When encountering obstacles (the things that don't feel good) ask yourself, "Is it my need for approval or my need for control that is getting in my way?" Once you identify one need, the other, or both, breathe and let go, breathe and let go. Return your attention to your authentic self.

5. GET RE-CENTERED, RECALIBRATE, GET PRESENT

Every time you stop to self-remember, self-observe, let go, and get centered you have successfully journeyed from head to heart. The present moment opens the door to your authenticity so you can access your creativity, wisdom, strength, and intuition. You are now able to be resourceful, re-Source-ful, *once–again–full–of–Source*. Breathe, reconnect, and replenish. When we are resourceful, a multitude of new options and resources become obvious, available, and accessible.

6. TAKE ALIGNED ACTION

When your actions (including your thoughts and words) are aligned with who you really are and what you want to create, you become powerful. You are no longer a victim. Your relationships will improve, your joy will return, your energy, creativity, wisdom, compassion, playfulness, curiosity, life purpose, and passion will all be accessible once again.

Whenever you feel disconnected, take these simple steps along your heart path.